Eversley Belfield

DEFY AND ENDURE
Great Sieges of Modern History

Crowell-Collier Press, New York

ACKNOWLEDGMENTS

I AM very greatly indebted to Miss Iris Oades, Warden of Chamberlain Hall, Southampton University, who translated for me so many passages from the German edition of Kara Mustafa's diary; the Hon. Mabel Strickland helped in several important matters connected with the Second Siege of Malta; Commander Denis Calnan RN gave me the benefit of his profound knowledge of the siege of St. Elmo. Thanks to the hospitality of Admiral and Mrs. Best, I was able to explore Gibraltar and its environs. The librarians and staff of both Southampton University and Prince Consort Libraries have, as always, been most helpful. Miss Thelma M. Nye of Batsfords has provided me with the kind of assistance every harassed author hopes to get from his publisher. Finally, my wife has consistently helped me by carefully reading the book in all its stages and has also put up with siege-like conditions while it was being written.

The map on page 13 was drawn by K. C. Jordan and reproduced by kind permission of The Folio Society Limited, and the maps on pages 8, 41, and 62 are details from maps drawn by Arthur Banks. Figures 16, 17, and 18 are from *The Illustrated London News*, 1870–1871.

Winchester, 1967   E.B.

Contents

Introduction
The Nature of Sieges

IMPORTANT SIEGES happen infrequently. Perhaps four or five times in any one century the special circumstances will arise that can lead to such an organized test of strength between two determined antagonists. Unlike a decisive battle campaign, a major siege demands an elaborate preparatory build-up and hence a quick victory is impossible. In this respect, a successful commander in the field may find himself repulsed by a relatively mediocer opponent; Wellington, for instance, hated siege warfare, and Napoleon avoided it as far as possible.

All major sieges involve places that are strategically of outstanding importance. This limits the field, since in practice only capital cities, like Vienna and Paris, or fortresses that command vital communication routes, like Malta and Gibraltar, are considered sufficiently valuable to risk the tremendous expense and effort that a major siege entails. For those attacking, the first essential is to seal off the besieged place from the outside world. This is always a laborious and often lengthy undertaking, and thus no government will embark upon a major siege without considerable thought, nor will it do so unless there seems to

be encouraging prospects of a relatively rapid success. At the start of many sieges, attractive surrender terms may be offered and any opportunities of exploiting signs of disunity among the besieged will be taken. Furthermore, once a siege has been begun, every device of cajolery, bribery, threats, and brute force will be employed to break the spirit of the defenders.

Both sides have to consider carefully the natural features as well as the physical size of the place to be besieged. If it is very small, its loss or capture will not repay the outlay in men and materials; on the other hand, if it is a very extensive place, it may prove impossible to invest it closely, or, alternatively, the defenders may not be able to garrison it strongly enough to resist for long. To assess the strength of the natural and the prepared defensive features of any well-fortified place is a very complex matter. Here history abounds in expensive mistakes; as will be seen, the Turks in the sixteenth century and the Germans in the twentieth century both underestimated the strength of Malta, while the Spanish and the French were too optimistic about their ability to capture Gibraltar in the eighteenth century. In general, natural fortresses, such as Malta and Gibraltar, nearly always seem to defeat the attacker, or cause terrible losses before being taken.

A second feature common to all famous sieges is the determination and endurance displayed by both sides. These qualities need to be particularly highly developed in the besieged, who must believe most strongly in the justice of their cause, as well as having faith in the ultimate success of their stand; fear may well play a great part in hardening the defenders' will to resist; this was most marked where irreconcilable religious differences existed, as in the sieges of Malta and Vienna.

In any siege, the defenders can be divided into one of two fairly distinct categories. In a purely military type of siege, like Malta in 1565, and Gibraltar, the garrison is composed largely of professional soldiers, with a few civilians, and thus both the antagonists have a similar background and outlook. In this sort of siege too, the problems of morale and discipline, being primarily of a military nature, are fairly simple. On the other hand, where the majority of those besieged are noncombatant men, women, and children, the difficulties of keeping up the spirits of these ordinary people can be most complex. Disease and hunger on a large scale can rapidly undermine even the strongest fortress, as Vienna discovered in 1683 and Paris in 1871; to accumulate enough stocks of food to feed over a million mouths for an indefinite period is an almost impossible task.

Sieges of very large cities are a most testing and democratic form of warfare because such a diverse cross-section of humanity is cooped up and cut off from all contact with the outside world. Whether they like it or not, all in the beleaguered city are directly affected. All suffer the same privations from hunger, all must share in that soul-destroying sense of boredom, which is so unnerving a feature of lengthy sieges, all have to withstand the common dangers, all are prone to catch the dreaded diseases that attend any siege, all are thrown back on their resources in a most acute manner, and, finally, all are exposed to the same fate if the city should fall into enemy hands. For those reading about wars, these sieges can appeal more directly to the experience of ordinary people, since the existence in a beleaguered city is really only the everyday world turned topsy-turvy. A siege brings out the best and the worst in those enduring it.

All great sieges have another distinctive feature: they reveal mercilessly the personalities of those in command. As the siege progresses, it can sometimes develop into a personal conflict between the two opposing leaders, as happened in the Great Siege of Malta. The heaviest burden lies upon the leader of the besieged, who, if he is to triumph, has to combine in himself a veritable galaxy of talents. He must be brave and appear to be brave without being foolhardy; he must have, or soon acquire, sufficient personal authority to be the unquestioned leader of his troops; he must be well versed in all the arts of conventional warfare, yet be sufficiently ingenious to achieve local surprises by employing new and improvised weapons; he must be ceaselessly vigilant, never normally accepting anything on trust, but he must also know when to have complete faith in the judgment of his subordinates; he must always be firm, though never arrogantly dictatorial; he must be quick to reward and encourage heroism, and quick to punish cowardice; such a man must remain serene in the face of setbacks and disappointments, so that he generates an air of confidence in eventual victory, but he must never give the impression that he is trying to buoy up hopes by putting on airs of false optimism; and, finally, he must, for this is an unsupportably lonely job, have a wise confidant to whom he can unburden himself and freely discuss the most intimate affairs of the siege.

From these accounts, it will be evident that La Valette fulfilled almost all these qualifications. Although a less endearing person, Eliott also possessed most of these rare qualities. At the opposite extreme was the feebleness shown during the siege of Paris, where it became more and more depressingly apparent that the French had no real leader.

On the side of the attackers, there emerged no dominating figures comparable with either La Valette or Eliott. In the Great Siege of Malta, even Dragut, the internationally famous Turkish commander, failed to come up to expectations, while Mustafa Pasha, the other leader, often acted more like a man driven by despair than a great general. The siege of Vienna revealed both the grave defects of Kara Mustafa's personal character and his lack of military experience. Only the crafty Bismarck managed to retain a fairly effective control over all the affairs connected with the siege of Paris, but, as has been mentioned, he really had no opponent worthy of note. As a generalization, it seems true to say that the circumstances under which the besieging forces have to operate do not bring out the finer qualities of leadership in their commanders. With all the complicated preparations involved, the conduct of a successful siege calls primarily for great administrative talents combined with relentless patience, foresight, and a methodical approach to the many problems which crop up; the emphasis is on im-

personal qualities that are alien to most great military leaders. In some strange way also, the commander of the investing troops suffers from a lack of stimulus, whereas adversity can bring out almost superhuman heroic qualities in the leader of the besieged forces.

In nearly every major siege, the intervention of outside forces is the vital factor. This is because, as both sides are well aware, those being besieged can resist from their own resources for only a limited time. It is this hope of relief that endows the besieged with the ultimate courage to stand firm against apparently hopeless odds, as in Malta in 1565 and Vienna in 1683. In both these cases, it was the last-minute arrival of powerful forces that broke the blockade and compelled the Turks to abandon the sieges. In contrast, once it was evident that no outside assistance would be forthcoming, the outcome of the siege of Paris was a foregone conclusion. In Gibraltar and Malta in the Second World War, the situation was somewhat different. A complete sea blockade is extremely difficult to maintain, and provided the British could muster sufficient naval forces to run convoys through to these places, there was no reason why they should not hold out indefinitely. Nevertheless, the regular resupplying of the more isolated Malta, with its 300,000 souls, was a far more complex problem than that of Gibraltar, where there were under 10,000 people.

In conclusion, the spirit of siege warfare was magnificently expressed by that fighting monarch Richard the Lion Heart. His great rival Philip Augustus boasted that he would capture the fortress castle of Chateau Gaillard even if its walls were made of steel; Richard replied that he would hold it even if its walls were made of butter.

The Great Siege of MALTA
May–September 1565

FROM MAY until September 1565 a small part of the island of Malta was besieged. Since then, this event has stirred the minds and imaginations of men and women all over the world. The reason for this interest lies in a fascinating and unusual combination of circumstances.

The Great Siege of Malta still remains one of the most remarkable examples of corporate heroism and determination. It was a unique example of calculated bravery against fearful odds. Less than 8,000 Christian soldiers (600 to 700 of whom were Knights of St. John), together with 1,000 local men, women, and children, resisted the violent and prolonged onslaughts of about 40,000 Turkish soldiers who were renowned as the most ferocious and experienced troops of their time. Very soon this conflict developed into a fight to the death. Once the still-warm and dripping heads of Turkish prisoners had been fired as cannon balls, a reprisal for Turkish atrocities, the defenders of Malta knew that they could expect no mercy if they surrendered. In the end about 7,000 out of the 9,000 defenders had been killed, while of the remaining 2,000 only 600 were ca-

pable of fighting. The Turkish losses were even more staggering, for it has been estimated that of the 40,000 soldiers engaged 25,000 eventually perished.

The drama of this siege was heightened by the fact that both sides were led by men of such outstanding character. The hero was undoubtedly La Valette, an aristocratic Frenchman from Provence who had joined the order at the age of 20 and had then dedicated his life to serving the needs of the Knights. In 1565 he was 70 years old, but his courage was still rock-like and his judgment unquestionable. Earlier in his eventful career he had spent a year as a Turkish galley slave, chained naked to a bench with six others, pulling at an enormous oar for up to 20 hours on end, often with no food except pieces of wine-soaked bread being shoved into his mouth at irregular intervals as he rowed. Only the most determined and resolute men survived a spell of this life, and La Valette was already 47 when his ship was captured and he was made a galley slave. This incredibly tough, but devout, old man transmitted his determination to the international

band of excitable, aristocratic, temperamental Knights of the Order of St. John who were under his command and formed the backbone of his troops. La Valette's right-hand man, his confidant and his secretary, was the sole Englishman in Malta, Sir Oliver Starkey.

The dominating figure on the Turkish side was even older. Dragut was 80 when he landed in Malta. His career can best be described as that of a free-lance pirate owing allegiance to the Sultan of Turkey. His reputation was based primarily on his incredible ability as a sea captain, but he was also a most able commander on land. By 1565 his fame almost eclipsed that of the great Barbarossa, who had trained him. Though known as the scourge of the Christians, he was a relatively humane man. Like La Valette, he too had been taken prisoner and worked as a Christian

galley slave. In this siege, Dragut operated at a considerable disadvantage. He did not arrive until after it had begun, when he found the command of the Turkish forces being acrimoniously shared between Admiral Piali, who was responsible for the fleet, and Mustafa Pasha, who was in charge of the land forces. If Dragut had been present from the beginning with the naval and land forces both under his control, the outcome of the siege might well have been different, since with the overwhelming forces at his disposal, he would almost certainly have overcome the garrison. These two men had been fighting against each other since youth, and this was to be the climax of their careers. Dragut perished as a result of the siege, while La Valette survived for another three years. As a memorial to his genius, the fine town of Valetta was built. Dragut is now commemorated only in the name of a spit of land known as Dragut Point, which guards the entrance to Sliema Harbor.

This siege was racked by suspense. The defenders were daily expecting relief from the viceroy of Sicily, but he kept postponing his decision to send aid. Thus those in Malta were left with no knowledge of whether they could expect help before it was too late. Every day was vital for La Valette and his companions because their small numbers were being steadily worn down by vigorous and fierce attacks. Even when the viceroy did send 10,000 men on August 25, misfortune struck the expedition. The fleet was dispersed by a storm. He managed to reassemble it, and on September 7 the first troops landed in Malta, with the garrison there at its last gasp.

On the outcome of this siege depended the fate of hundreds of thousands who were unaware of what was happening at the time. If the Turks had secured Malta in 1565, their fleets could have dominated not only the eastern, but also the western half of the Mediterranean. Based on the magnificent and safe Grand Harbor of Malta, Turkish raiding parties could have operated from there and roamed around the coasts of Sicily and Italy seizing men, women, and children to make them slaves of the Turkish empire.

Finally, from the wider point of view, this siege was a part of the prolonged struggle between Christians and Turks, which went back over four and a half centuries to the Crusades. Up to 1565 the Turks had been almost continuously successful in this bloodthirsty and widespread conflict with the forces of Christendom. Despite the enormous preparations they had made to conquer the relatively ill-fortified island of Malta, this was the first major setback to Turkish arms, and the world was astounded at their failure.

The Maltese people had not been thrown into this war with the Turks on their own account. The story of their unwilling involvement goes back to 1530, when the Emperor Charles V had presented Malta to the homeless Knights of St. John. In 1523, the Turks had driven the Knights out of the larger and richer island of Rhodes, which had been their home for over two centuries. At first the Knights had not taken kindly to the relatively barren Malta and had done little to fortify their base, which they had established in the magnificent harbor whose existence had been the main reason for their grudging acceptance of Charles' gift. With the election in 1557 of La Valette as the Grand Master, a systematic effort was begun to prepare the island against the next major round of the Knights' running battle with the Turkish empire. When the Knights continued to harry the Turks' shipping as effectively from Malta as they had done earlier from Rhodes, a serious showdown between the two protagonists became inevitable.

Officially recognized by the Papacy in 1113, the Knights Hospitallers of St. John of Jerusalem was as unusual a body of men as the world has ever seen. Originally founded as a peaceable nursing organization to provide hospitals and care for the physical needs of the sick pilgrims to the Holy Land, it had developed into one of the most snobbish, courageous, and warlike cliques imaginable. By the fourteenth century the Knights had become permanently engaged in trying to stem the power of the Turkish empire, and specialized in sea warfare. Being directly under the protection of the Papacy, they were independent of the ruler of Europe. Organized on a language basis, the order was divided into eight tongues (*langues*), those of Auvergne, Provence, France, Aragon, Castile, England, Germany, and Italy, each having

2 *A general view of the Siege from an engraving made after the original of Mateo Perez d' Aleccio, first published by Lucini in 1631*

A *Fort St. Angelo*
B *Birgu*
C *Bormla*
D *St. Michael*
E *Santa Margarita*
F *The Belvedere*
G *The Mandra*
H *Corradino Heights*
I   *Boats being transported from Marsamuscetto*
K *Two batteries bombarding Birgu*
L *A battery bombarding St. Angelo*
M *Two batteries bombarding St. Elmo*
N *St. Elmo*
O *Mount Calcara*
P *Gallows Point*
Q *Manoel Island*
R *Mount Salvador*
S *Dragut Point*
T *Marsamuscetto*
V *Artillery being disembarked*
X *The ford to Manoel Island*
Y *The chain sealing off Grand Harbor*
Z *Paulo Micho's vineyard*

its own headquarters in Malta; by 1565 the French element dominated the others. The order was ruled by the military knights, who were recruited solely from the great aristocratic houses; one essential qualification for entry being noble birth on both sides of the family for four generations. Many of these nobles, however, only joined the order for a brief period. They served as the officers in the warships or galleys, to gain firsthand experience of this particular type of fighting, and then returned to their great estates, from whose wealth the order benefited. On the other hand, some of these great nobles, like La Valette, took their vows of chastity and obedience seriously and made maritime warfare against the Turks their lifelong profession, becoming a match for their enemy in this form of warfare, which demanded an incredible mixture of toughness, bravery, and skill. The two lower groups in the order were the chaplains and the serving brothers, who were professional soldiers; neither of these classes needed to be of noble birth and they had no say in the running of affairs.

Once a Knight always a Knight. When the order faced an emergency the Grand Master could recall the nonserving Knights. La Valette sent out this summons to rejoin in 1564. This elite officer band brought with them their immediate retainers, who, together with the permanent serving brothers, formed the core of "other ranks" fighting strength of the order. In addition the order had recruited several thousand mercenary soldiers, mainly Spaniards and Italians, hardened professionals, like the sixty-year-old Francisco Balbi di Correggio from whose chronicle most accounts of the siege are drawn.

Without three things, such an order would have withered away. First its members had to be inspired by a faith. The Knights found this in a most militant form of Catholicism. Secondly they had to have a foe; this role the Turkish empire filled. Thirdly the Knights had to possess some home where they could follow their own laws and policies unhindered by any national overlord. In this respect, they came reluctantly to recognize that Malta suited their purpose admirably, since it was strategically better placed than Rhodes. Although only seventeen miles long and nowhere more than eight miles wide, Malta was not easy to capture, since being composed of solid rock any attacker was confronted with great difficulty in mining under its fortifications, a major hazard in siege warfare at this period. With a rocky coastline rising up sheer for 300 to 400 feet, Malta's long southward side is virtually impregnable. On its other sides, it presents a flatter face to the sea, and there are several wide bays.

For the Knights, Malta's greatest asset consisted in its fine large deep-water harbor. This is protected by both a narrow entrance and a long tongue of high land, then known as Mount Sciberras, which splits the harbor into two unequal parts. The bigger of these two divisions is called the Grand Harbor, and nestling inside it are three small creeks about one hundred yards broad; they run inland between two finger-like promontories, the outer one known as Birgu and the inner one called Senglea.

Due to the Knights' original aversion to settling permanently in Malta, the great potential strength of the Grand Harbor had not been fully exploited, even by 1565. A star-shaped fort called St. Elmo had, however, been nearly completed at the tip of Mount Sciberras, and guarded the entrance to the harbor mouth. This fort suffered from a very grave defect, because it was entirely

overlooked by the higher ground of Mount Sciberras, at this date unoccupied. On the south side of the harbor, both the peninsulas of Birgu and Senglea had been partially fortified by walls, but they were also dominated by the higher ground inland, which had not been fortified and anyhow could not have been held by the small forces at the Knights' disposal. Finally at the tip of Birgu peninsula the well-situated and substantial fort of St. Angelo, which dated back to Norman times, had been strengthened. It commanded a wide stretch of the Grand Harbor, and its upper guns covered most of Mount Sciberras across the harbor water about half a mile away. Considerably bigger than St. Elmo, St. Angelo was separated from Birgu by a small ditch with a drawbridge; it would have been possible for all the garrison to have retired into St. Angelo, but having no water storage tanks, it could not have withstood a prolonged siege.

After 1557, more and more Turkish vessels were captured by the Knights, who towed them into the safety of their lairs inside the Grand Harbor. In 1563 a great ship full of valuable goods was brought intact into the Grand Harbor; a big share in this ship's cargo was held by the chief eunuch to the Sultan Soleyman, and many of his harem also had shares in its rich contents. These voices shrilly joined the chorus which had for long been urging the seventy-year-old Sultan to teach the Knights a final lesson, and he now decided to destroy their power for ever.

During the winter of 1564–65 the Turks were preparing for their attack on Malta. By March 22 a fleet of over 250 vessels had been assembled off Constantinople; among the stores these vessels carried were over 60 pieces of assault artillery, the largest weighing 9 tons and firing a colossal

marble cannon ball of 112 pounds; stowed on board also were dozens of smaller guns that fired iron cannon balls of 56 pounds. On 10 of the larger ships alone were carried 100,000 iron cannon balls and 75 tons of gunpowder. As well as the military equipment, the Turks had to ship with them vast quantities of food, since about 40,000 troops and 25,000 sailors and slaves had to be supplied, there being no food available in Malta itself. In addition, several hundred horses were taken. The organization, loading, assembling, and conveying of this enormous fleet was one of the most massive and impressive invasion enterprises that has ever been undertaken, and bears comparison with the same kind of operations that were mounted by the Allies in the Second World War. When this armada arrived at Navarino in Greece it was joined by other vessels. The whole force then set out for Malta on May 12.

On Friday, May 18, the contemporary chronicler Balbi reported, "Our watchmen on St. Angelo and St. Elmo sighted the Turkish fleet 30 miles to the southeast. As soon as it was seen, the prearranged signal was given for the inhabitants to take shelter inside the fortifications, and 2 guns were fired to warn Medina [the ancient hilltop capital of the island] and Gozo [the smaller neighboring island three miles north of Malta]. Immediately, the islanders rushed to Birgu, bringing with them their children, their cattle, and their possessions. Not wishing all these refugees to enter Birgu, the Grand Master diverted some to Senglea, which was less fortified.

"As the fleet neared the island, it was seen to be making for Marsa Xlokk. This is a large harbor five miles from Birgu, and safe in all winds except the Sirocco. When he saw their objective, the Grand Master dispatched the marshal from Birgu to oppose them." In all 1,000 fighting men, including 100 Knights, went there.

"When the Turkish fleet was so close to the shore that they could see our troops, they realized that they could not make an unopposed landing, so with a fresh breeze in their sails, they took a southerly course along the island. Our men followed them on foot and on horseback until nightfall."

The Knights could not long prevent the Turks making a landing, and their fleet returned to Marsa Xlokk, where on May 20 the Turkish troops came ashore in strength. By the following day they had moved 4 miles inland to the Marsa, a low-lying piece of ground at the head of the Grand Harbor, which had a good supply of water though the springs there had been contaminated as a part of La Valette's scorched-earth policy.

On May 21 a large battle took place. Balbi recounts:

"The Turks now made a large-scale demonstration in front of us, in order to reconnoiter Birgu and also frighten us with great numbers, for they were more than 40,000. Realizing their intention the Grand Master gave orders for all our drums to be beaten and for all our flags to be unfurled. When the moment seemed ripe he sent out 600 to 700 arquebusiers. At the same time Captain Guaras charged out with the cavalry and a fierce engagement took place. . . .

"The Grand Master held over 1,000 men ready in reserve, he himself standing inside the gate with a lance in his hand to prevent reserves from rushing into battle without orders. Had he not been there to hold them back, he would not have found a single man in Birgu, so great was their desire to get at the enemy.

"This engagement lasted for five hours, at the end of which La Valette ordered his forces to retire." Though the Knights had inflicted comparatively heavy casualties on the Turks, the Grand Master could not afford to risk dissipating his small forces in this kind of action.

Two days after their landing, the joint Turkish leaders Mustafa and Piali held a momentous council of war. There was a deep difference of opinion between them as to where to attack first. Mustafa Pasha, the commander of the land forces, rightly wanted to bombard the Knights' main stronghold at Birgu and Senglea immediately. This was to be a holding operation, conducted by himself, while a strong detachment under Piali was to be sent to capture Medina, the ill-fortified ancient capital of Malta, which is perched on a steep hill and overlooks most of the island. Having taken Medina, his plan was to seize the rest of the unfortified places in Malta before invading the helpless island of Gozo. Thus Malta would have been effectively sealed off first, before the Turks concentrated all their resources into battering the Knights' tiny strong points into submission. As Balbi commented, "If Mustafa's advice had been followed, we should certainly have been lost, for all our reliefs reached us by way of Medina. But Almighty God did not permit that it should be so, for it was His will that the two pashas in their jealousy should disagree violently with one another—as we learned from deserters."

Piali was the naval commander, and the Sultan had unwisely given the two men equal authority over the expedition. Piali's first concern was for the safety of his vast fleet, and, in his opinion, Marsa Xlokk harbor was not a safe enough anchorage. After an argument, Mustafa conceded that the first objective should be the seizure of St. Elmo, since once it was taken Piali's fleet could anchor, immune from storms, in Marsamuscetto, the undefended part of the best harbor in the island.

Everything occurred at such close quarters that the defenders could watch and hear much of what was going on. In Balbi's words, "Friday, May 25. The enemy now began to transport their main artillery from the fleet to St. Elmo. This was a very difficult task, for the guns were heavy, their wheels and carriages were made of iron, and they had to take them a distance of 9 miles over rocky and stony ground. Unfortunately the serfs and beasts of burden that the Maltese had left behind in the countryside (despite the Grand Master's orders) proved of the greatest help. From the spur of St. Michael (in Senglea) we could see 10 to 12 oxen, as well as many men, harnessed to ropes pulling the guns."

As soon as he realized the Turks intentions La Valette did all he could to strengthen St. Elmo. "When the Turks attacked the fort, there were 800 fighting men defending it. He provisioned the garrison with biscuits, wine, cheese, salt pork, vegetables, oil, and vinegar . . . and cattle, which

had been kept in the ditch around the fort. . . . The Grand Master also sent over powder, lead, rope, combustibles, and explosive fireworks."

Simultaneously the defense walls of Birgu and Senglea were being improved. One minor problem was that everyone had brought his dog with him, and their barking at night disturbed the sentries. La Valette had all dogs destroyed, including his own hunting dogs, which he loved. No matter was too trivial to escape his disciplined watchfulness.

The Grand Master would very soon need all his authority; 48 hours after the beginning of the bombardment of St. Elmo, a Knight from there entered the council chamber when La Valette was presiding over a meeting. Although only ordered to ask for reinforcements, he painted a despairing picture of life in St. Elmo, maintaining that it could not hope to resist for more than another eight days. La Valette was furious. He humiliated the Knight publicly by offering to go himself at the head of a group of volunteers, but was dissuaded from this extreme measure. Instead he sent 50 Knights and 200 soldiers, all volunteers, to reinforce St. Elmo. La Valette well knew that St. Elmo was doomed. But the longer it held out, the more time there was to strengthen the defenses of Birgu and Senglea and thereby improve the chances of Malta holding out until the promised relief force arrived from Sicily.

The Turkish experts had predicted that St. Elmo would fall within a week. Nevertheless it was holding out as strongly as ever, when on June 2 Dragut arrived, bringing with him yet more troops and guns. He saw at once that it had been a terrible error attacking St. Elmo first, especially when the Turkish forces were being harassed by cavalry raids from the unsubdued garrison in Medina. But by now the abandonment of the St. Elmo siege would have been a severe blow to Turkish morale, and Dragut had to accept the situation as it was. He did, however, infuse new vigor and greater skill into the siege. On Tigne Point, at the westward entrance to the main harbor, he installed some heavy guns to hammer away at the walls of St. Elmo from another angle; this speeded up the process of reducing the fortress to rubble. Surprisingly, La Valette had found that he was able to supply and reinforce the garrison under the cover of darkness and, on the return trip, ferry out the badly wounded, thus sparing the defenders the demoralizing task of tending their disabled in the midst of battle. Determined to end this invaluable system of keeping the garrison up to strength with fresh men and material, Dragut ordered a wall to be built from the top of Mount Sciberras to the water's edge, so enabling the Turks to approach the St. Elmo landing stage unobserved by the alert gunners on St. Angelo. He also positioned guns on Gallows Point (at the other entrance to the harbor), which could both pound the fort and rake its sole landing place with fire.

In St. Elmo itself, during the first week of June, the Turks seized the ravelin, or protective outworks, and thus could start to storm the walls. They made a scaffolding bridge to span the ditch and rested it against the main western wall; in spite of their desperate efforts, the garrison failed to destroy or burn down this contraption. From their many vantage places, Turkish snipers picked off sentries and fired at anyone who moved. All the time, the bombardment continued relentlessly, daily 6,000 to 7,000 iron and marble cannon balls were hurled at the fort, and its soft-stoned walls were steadily being pulverized.

3   Detail from engraving of the Attack on St. Elmo. A skirmish outside Birgu in which the Knights were victorious.

On June 7, there was another major attack. "To the watchers on St. Angelo, it seemed as if St. Elmo's last hour had come. Smoke and dust clouds trembled over the headland; cannon balls ricocheting off the walls screamed skywards to fall into the sea; vast lumps of masonry detaching themselves from the ramparts boomed down the steep rock face on the eastern side and crashed into the Grand Harbor. It was incredible that anything could live in such a tempest."

Yet when the attack came ". . . it was met with a hail of bullets and incendiary weapons." The Turks were driven off eventually, but covered their retreat with "such devastating fire . . . that the defenders could neither man their guns nor take any action against the retreating Turks."

Although this tremendous attack had been successfully repulsed, the Grand Master was faced by another sort of crisis in St. Elmo itself. Realizing the hopelessness of their situation and naturally not wishing to be slaughtered like trapped animals, the Knights there "begged La Valette to give them permission to sally out and fight in the open." In the meantime, La Valette had heard help was on its way from Sicily and was promised for

June 20. This meant that all defensible positions had to be held to the last. The Grand Master dealt shrewdly with this semimutiny. He offered to withdraw all the garrison from St. Elmo, replacing them with volunteers from the Birgu and Senglea forces. His message stated, "I shall feel more confident when I know that the fort upon which the safety of the island so greatly depends is held by men whom I can trust implicitly." La Valette knew what the immediate reaction would be to this thinly veiled charge of cowardice. The Knights felt keenly shamed. Their honor was at stake. They had vowed to defend the order to death. Unanimously they agreed to stay and fight, although they hated the prospect of having to die like rats in a trap instead of in the open like fighting men.

To the consternation of the Turks and to the pride and surprise of the onlookers 1,000 yards away across the Grand Harbor, the gallant garrison of St. Elmo held out for another two weeks. Not only was the fort subjected to frequent full-scale attacks by day, but on June 10 there was a night assault. Balbi described the effect, "The immense number of flares and incendiaries used by both sides meant that there was no darkness. We who were in the garrison of St. Michael (in Senglea) could see Fort St. Elmo quite clearly, while the gunners in St. Angelo and the other positions were able to lay their guns by the light of the enemy's fires."

On June 18, Dragut's protective wall was finished. It ran from the top of Mount Sciberras right down to the shores of the Grand Harbor below the fort. St. Elmo was now completely sealed off.

On June 22 what was intended as the final assault began. This time the Knights across the water in St. Angelo had to withhold their supporting fire, since both sides were so enmeshed that they could not distinguish friend from foe. Balbi reported of the Turks that "they did not confine themselves to one place, but laid their scaling ladders against the walls at every point on the fort's circumference. There was not a single place where there was not some fighting going on." The struggle continued for six hours in the grilling heat of midsummer. Then, to the astonishment of the sorrowing onlookers, cheers were heard coming from within St. Elmo. Once more the Turks had been driven off, and their losses were estimated at 2,000. About 200 of the 300 defenders also lay dead. But on this day the Turks suffered a disaster. Dragut was calmly superintending the installation of some guns, in full view of the batteries of St. Angelo, when a cannon ball from there narrowly missed him, splintering a nearby rock, and jagged splinters hit him on the head. At first thought to be dead, he survived just long enough to be told of the fall of St. Elmo.

That night an experienced Maltese swimmer crossed the warm waters of the Grand Harbor to enter the crumbling fort. In Balbi's words, "The messenger said that there was not a man left in St. Elmo who was not covered with his own blood as well as that of the enemy, and they had no ammunition left at all." La Valette was so moved he wept, and impulsively agreed to try to run relief boats through the blockade to St. Elmo. Filled with volunteers, five boats set out, but the Turks had anticipated this effort. The boats were met by such concentrated fire that they were compelled to return.

Now the garrison prepared for death. The two chaplains heard the confessions and gave Holy Communion to everyone. In a touching "last gesture, and as a signal to their friends and brethren in St. Angelo, Birgu, and Senglea that they had made peace and were ready for the end, they began ringing the bell of the small chapel."

On June 23, the Turkish troops advanced to finish off the garrison. Even this proved more difficult than they had expected, taking an hour's hard fighting. Typical of the bravery shown was the behavior of two Knights who were so severely wounded that they could not even stand. They sat in chairs, each armed with a two-handed sword, and fought until they were hacked to pieces. A few Maltese plunged into the harbor to escape by swimming to Birgu, and nine wounded Knights were captured and hidden by the corsairs, who hoped to obtain a large ransom for them. The rest perished.

Fort St. Elmo stands about 100 feet above the water and, though rebuilt, its main outline is little altered. From tip to tip of its star-shape, St. Elmo measures less than 250 yards and, at its broadest, it extends for about 150 yards; the only open space inside being a small square about the size of two tennis courts. Yet this minute fort held out for 31 days against scores of guns and cost the Turks at least 8,000 dead and nearly 20,000 wounded; 1,500 of the defenders were killed and about 4,000 wounded. Surveying the 1,500 dead and decomposing bodies strewn around St. Elmo and comparing its tiny size with that of Birgu and Senglea, Mustafa Pasha lamented, "Allah! If so small a son has cost us so dear, what price shall we have to pay for so large a father?"

For the three weeks from June 24 to July 14 there was an interlude. The Turkish forces were getting set for their mighty assault on the Knights' strong holds at Birgu and Senglea. Before it started, the Turks decided to teach the defenders a macabre lesson. "They secured to planks and pieces of wood the bodies of the Christian dead—some mutilated, some without heads, and others with their bellies ripped open—and threw them into the sea so that the current would wash them over to Birgu." The plan misfired, ". . . for the sight of our dead friends roused in us [the Knights] a desire for vengeance." This took the barbarous form of firing at their enemy the heads of freshly decapitated Turkish prisoners.

A high-ranking deserter confirmed the Grand Master's opinion that the first attack would be against Senglea and would be launched partly from the landward side and partly from vessels approaching from the Grand Harbor. Senglea was particularly vulnerable to the Turks on the Corradino Heights, a mere quarter of a mile away across the narrow French Creek. These surrounding hills were soon ringed with Turkish guns, many dragged there from Mount Sciberras, while other batteries were repositioned to concentrate their fire across the Grand Harbor into Senglea. To the horror of the defenders, Turkish vessels suddenly appeared at the top end of the Grand Harbor. Not daring to run the gauntlet of the batteries at St. Angelo, the Turks had resorted to a cunning device used once or twice before in such an emergency. With the aid of great wooden rollers, teams of galley slaves and oxen, under the lash of whips, had hauled 80 ships of various sizes half a mile overland, from the upper reaches of Marsamucetto Harbor right over the top of the rocky Mount Sciberras and down into the waters of the Grand Harbor.

In the meantime the Knights were using their respite to work feverishly on strengthening their defenses, especially on the landward side of Senglea. Slaves were put to work on the more exposed positions, being sent out chained in pairs. Inside Birgu and Senglea, "The sick and disabled slaves were kept busy the whole time making fuses. . . . Night and day our blacksmiths' forges were working on repairs, to guns as well as making nails." The night was sometimes enlivened by name-calling matches between the two sides, but on learning about these verbal exchanges of fire, the Grand Master ordered that the garrison should remain silent in spite of the provocation.

During this comparative lull, La Valette greatly improved the defenses by two well-conceived measures. First he had a bridge of boats built across Dockyard Creek to link Birgu and Senglea. With the land communications cut, this bridge permitted the garrisons, when the need arose, to reinforce each other speedily. A great chain stretching across the lower end of Dockyard Creek kept the bridge safe from enemy seaborne raids, but being within the range of Turkish batteries, it often had to be repaired, and those crossing by it were always liable to be shot at.

Secondly the Grand Master had a row of very large stakes driven into the waters of French Creek. Running parallel with the Senglea peninsula, and about a dozen yards out, these prevented any boats reaching the shore. Thus any waterborne attackers would be compelled to wade ashore, getting their clothes and their powder wet as well as being directly exposed to the fire of the defenders behind the Senglea wall. Naturally the Turks reacted to this obstacle. Protected by the fire from snipers on the Corradino Heights, some swimmers were despatched with axes to cut down the poles and wires that linked them. When this valuable defense seemed doomed, some Maltese plunged into the water armed with knives and swords. A series of individual fights ensued, but the more effectively armed Maltese attacked so ferociously that the Turks fled. The next day Mustafa sent boats out with cables that were secured to the stakes; the cables were then brought back to capstans on the other side of the creek, where gangs of slaves began to wind them out of the water. The dismayed garrison watched until some daring Maltese swam out and hacked through the cables.

Before being subjected to nearly seven weeks of incessant attacks, the Knights had been immeasurably heartened and strengthened by the arrival of a small group of reinforcements. These troops arrived at the north of the island the very day St. Elmo fell. Very careful arrangements had to be made to pass them unseen through the Turkish lines. After a long night march on June 29, in which a thick mist helped to shroud and muffle their movements, these 700 fresh and well-trained troops reached Kalkara Creek and were ferried silently into Birgu.

The Knights and their supporters were now almost completely cut off in Senglea and Birgu. From July 15 to August 7, these two garrisons endured an almost continuous succession of fierce Turkish assaults. The first, and one of the most determined of these attacks, was directed against Senglea only. On July 15 Mustafa threw many of his best troops into the battle. One group was led by the newly arrived viceroy of Algiers, a son-in-law of Dragut who had infuriated Mustafa by scornfully remarking of St. Elmo that "he could not understand how it could possibly have held out for so long."

The first wave of these attackers came across the water from the Marsa. They were preceded for part of the way by three boats on which Imams (Moslem holy men) stood chanting texts from the Koran.

Balbi was defending a section of the wall here and recalled, "The sun was now up and we could see the boats more clearly. Their sides were built up with sacks of wool and cotton, and they were lined with magnificent-looking troops. . . . Even the rank and file wore scarlet robes, and there were many in cloth of gold and of silver and of crimson damask. Armed with the fine muskets of Fez, scimitars of Alexandria and Damascus, and magnificent bows, they all wore splendid turbans."

On approaching the line of stakes and chains, the oarsmen put on a spurt, but failed to break the barrier. The soldiers sprang into the water and began to swim and wade ashore. Though met by concentrated fire, this mass of warriors reached the low walls with their scaling ladders. Very soon the Turks had gained a foothold. The defenders, whose guns had been put out of action earlier by accurate enemy fire, now suffered another calamity—a powder magazine blew up and the explosion brought down some of the wall. The Turks took advantage of this misfortune and charged in.

Balbi was in the thick of it. "We were so few in number that we found it better to lay aside our arquebuses and hurl rocks at them. In this way we could do them more harm and hit them more often." Of one of the Knights, he wrote, "The Turks recognized him as a leader by his armor and colorful trappings . . . they opened fire on him and hit him. . . . Luckily his breastplate was bulletproof and he was unharmed. But soon after this, a Janissary, wearing a large black headdress with gold ornaments on it, knelt at the foot of the battery, aimed upwards at him, and shot him in the groin. . . . The Turks, seeing the Knight fall, set up a shout of joy, as they always did when they killed a man of any note." A fantastic tug-of-war followed, in which the Turks grabbed the dead man's legs while Balbi and his companions hung on to his arms until "we got the body away from them, but not before they had pulled off the shoes from his feet." The soldiers were most anxious to retain the dead Knight, since the Turks decapitated important corpses and impaled their heads on stakes; a row of these grisly objects gaped at the garrison day and night.

Meanwhile, a separate Turkish attack had developed against the landward walls of Senglea. Violent though it was, the defenders there managed to keep it fairly successfully at bay. But those defending the seawalls were now at their last gasp. La Valette realized their plight and, using his bridge of boats, he rushed a contingent of fresh troops from Birgu to save them.

Almost simultaneously Mustafa sent in the third wave of his troops, which he intended should take the defenders of Senglea in the rear by surprise. Ten galleys of Janissaries, the "crack" formations of the Turkish army, set off quietly across the Grand Harbor. They were to land on Birgu, just above the huge chain that barred the entrance to the Dockyard Creek. They had, however, been observed by the alert commander of a battery of five guns, stationed below the castle of St. Angelo. Specially positioned to deal with any attack of this kind, this battery had not been spotted by the Turks, and its commander waited until the boats neared the land, where he could not miss them. Loaded with shot, pieces of chain, and iron caltrops (four spiked iron balls), he ordered his battery to fire salvos. All the Turkish boats were sunk, and their troops, chosen because they could not swim, were either drowned or killed as they struggled ashore. The diversionary attack had thus ended in complete failure.

After five hours of the most desperate fighting, Mustafa abandoned the attack. About 3,000 of the Turkish attackers had perished, the garrisons' losses being about 250. That night, and for some time afterward, the good swimmers collected a rich harvest. The harbor was strewn with Turkish corpses, which were systematically stripped of jewelry, rings, purses, and finely decorated personal weapons. Hashish was also found in considerable quantities; probably many of the attackers had been given drugs to fill them with fanatical courage. In many of the sunken ships were found large quantities of food, proving that the Turks had expected to capture the Senglea peninsula and settle there.

Although so heavily repulsed, the Turkish forces persisted in attacking almost daily for the next three weeks. They also tried to wear the defenders down by a relentless bombardment, which continued almost 'round the clock and which was directed chiefly at two places. One was the landward wall of Senglea, at St. Michael's post, which the Turks had failed to overrun in their first great attack. Here they even tunneled through the solid rock and drove two shafts in under the walls; the longer, packed with explosives, was intended to blow a gap in the walls. The other shaft was designed to pass troops in under the walls themselves. But the sentries were alert and noticed a subsidence in the loose earth. A party of men immediately investigated, found the entrance to this tunnel, and drove the Turks out of it; they also discovered the mine shaft and destroyed it.

The other place on which the Turks concentrated was the post of Castile, where the land-

4 *Detail from the Siege of St. Michael*

A *Fort St. Angelo*
E *The chain*
K *The galleon captured by the Turks*
L *The bridge linking Birgu and the island*
M *The second chain*
P *A battery bombarding Birgu and*
    St. Angelo
Q *Dragut Point*

ward wall of Birgu came closest to Senglea. Opposite both the St. Michael post in Senglea and the post of Castile, trenches were dug up to the walls to protect the attacking troops. In addition, the enemy artillery pounded away at the walls, which were crumbling slowly in spite of energetic repair work. This bombardment reached a climax on August 2 when "so great was the noise that in Syracuse and Catania (in Sicily), the one seventy and the other one hundred miles from Malta, the inhabitants heard the sound—like the distant rumble of thunder." The weary garrisons then repulsed Turkish attacks for six hours. Yet Mustafa refused to give up and decided to give the Knights five more days of heavy bombardment to soften them up further.

On August 7 the Turkish commanders reckoned that the time had come to make another all-out effort, simultaneously against Birgu and Senglea. These onslaughts continued for nine hours, in the grilling midsummer heat, and only ceased because of an unforeseen intervention.

At Birgu the Turks achieved an apparently overwhelming advantage when they breached the outer walls. But they were then unexpectedly confronted by another wall, which had been built to meet just such an emergency. Bottled up between the two walls, they were subjected to intense crossfire from muskets and cannon and also from fearsome incendiary weapons. The Knights specialized in these missiles, the most ingenious of which were hoops about the thickness of a man's leg. They took a lot of preparing, since they were "composed of the lightest wood, and were first dipped into brandy, then rubbed with oil, and then covered with wool and cotton which had been baked in other combustible liquors as well as mixed with saltpeter and gunpowder . . .

when the hoops were on fire, they were taken up with tongs and thrown into the midst of the advancing battalions. Two or three soldiers would regularly get entangled with one of these blazing hoops." With their long flowing robes, the Turkish soldiers were particularly vulnerable to these contraptions.

The defenders also used a crude sort of hand grenade, made by filling light earthenware pots with an inflammable mixture known as wildfire. These could be thrown twenty to thirty yards and, with the fuses lit, would explode on impact. Known as trumps, tubes of wood or metal were filled with wildfire and attached to long poles. Lit by a fuse and thrust into the enemy ranks, trumps acted as miniature flamethrowers and "continued a long time snorting and belching vivid, furious flames."

Large stones, cauldrons of boiling oil, pitch, or even scalding water were sometimes thrown or poured on to the heads of the enemy as they attempted to scale the walls. Several hours of this murderous kind of retaliation proved too much for the Turks attacking Birgu on August 7, and they had to withdraw. The garrison sallied out to finish off as many of the retreating Turks as they could, but they dared not venture beyond the walls for fear of a counterattack.

The 70-year-old Mustafa personally led a determined assault on Senglea. He appreciated, as did the garrison, that on this occasion no help could be spared from the Birgu garrison. After several hours of violent conflict, the Turks seemed about to break right through, but, at the crucial moment, La Valette himself entered the fray. His presence helped rally the desperate defenders, and once more the enemy were temporarily driven off. Nevertheless Mustafa still had fresh troops, the famous Janissaries, whom he was holding in reserve, and they now appeared ready to deliver the final decisive blow. But suddenly, when victory appeared inevitable, Mustafa called off his men. There was no apparent reason for this action. The exhausted garrison were astounded by this turn of events.

Their apparently miraculous deliverance had been brought about by the governor of Medina. As he heard the din and watched the smoke erupting from both Birgu and Senglea, he realized the gravity of the situation and decided to risk all to help La Valette. He collected his entire cavalry force, and they dashed off down the long slope to the Turkish camp at Marsa, some seven miles away. As he had anticipated it was very lightly guarded. The few sentries were quickly overwhelmed. The horsemen then set about killing the wounded, destroying the stores, slaughtering the animals, and burning the tents. From the accounts of the terrified survivors of this massacre, the Turks assumed that a large relief force had unexpectedly arrived. The attack on Senglea was thus broken off. When he realized how he had been tricked, Mustafa tore his beard in fury and swore he would have his revenge. Throughout mid-August a relentless pressure was kept up against the weary, weakened garrisons in Senglea and Birgu. In both peninsulas, this steady bombardment was reducing the landward walls to little more than heaps of rubble in many places; over 70,000 cannon shots being fired at the defenses, many at almost point-blank range.

In this period of remorseless conflict the Turks exploded an enormous mine under the walls of Birgu. The garrison had known that tunneling might be going on, since the stone thereabouts was soft enough for slaves to carve through it. But the noise of the gunfire was so continuous that the garrison was unable to locate the direction of this shaft. When this mine did go up, the explosion temporarily threw the defenders off their balance. It was touch-and-go whether the Turks would succeed in rushing through the breach in the walls and into the town itself. Once again the Grand Master came to the rescue. With his small bodyguard he hurled himself into the midst of the fighting. His bravery helped turn the scales, and the attack was repulsed; nevertheless, before this had happened La Valetta had been wounded in the leg, but he insisted on remaining in the thick of the fray until the situation was restored.

To exploit this breach the Turks next resorted to a favorite device. They constructed a tall tower, shrouding it in huge sheets of leather, which were regularly doused with water to render them impervious to incendiaries. This lofty affair was dragged up close to the remains of the wall so that snipers from its top storey could pick off all who showed themselves in this part of Birgu. The situation soon became critical. This tower had to be destroyed quickly, and, as in so many other crises, the Grand Master saved the day by his ingenuity. He ordered a hole to be dug through the bottom of a section of the main wall, and into this was moved a large gun. The last few stones were taken out very cautiously, and the cannon was edged forward so that its muzzle was just clear of the wall. Fortunately the Turks perched up aloft could observe little or nothing of what was going on almost directly below them. This gun was loaded with chain-shot, which whirled through the air with a scythe-like effect (chain-shot consisted of two cannon balls fastened together by a chain and was often employed in sea battles to bring down the enemy's rigging and masts). The chain-shot soon began to undermine the legs of the tower, and its heavy superstructure crashed down, throwing out the startled occupants. The gun was now speedily dragged back, and the hole in the wall sealed up.

By now the strain on the Grand Master must have been overwhelming. All accounts are unanimous in praising his personal courage, his resourcefulness, his foresight, his blend of military and human wisdom, his care for all the garrison, his resolution, and above all his fervent religious faith, which supported an unshakable conviction in the justice of his cause. Without his dominating personality, it is doubtful whether the garrison could have held out, especially during those last grim weeks, when all hope of relief had vanished.

La Valette's wisdom was wonderfully displayed when the Grand Council suggested that all the fighting members of the garrison should finally withdraw into Fort St. Angelo. As so often before, the Grand Master spotted the military weakness of this suggestion, which would have permitted the Turks to concentrate all their forces, in a way so far denied to them, against one small position. Standing alone, St. Angelo would thus have been doomed. He refused therefore to consider this forlorn plan, and instead sternly ordered the drawbridge connecting St. Angelo to Birgu to be destroyed. This most aristocratic of men also showed a feeling towards the common people very rare in this age. He would never consider the ordinary Maltese men, women, and children being sacrificed, when they had so bravely identified themselves with the Knights' cause by sharing in all the privations of the siege. Balbi, too, was most impressed by both the strength and hu-mility of this great man, and wrote of him, "There was no type of work from which he spared himself, whether physical or mental, in keeping us on our toes and ready for every emergency. He would sleep in the most exposed positions and made night rounds constantly, even though the knights in charge begged him not to risk his life, but to take care of himself." La Valette's attention to practical details must have made all the difference between success or failure when the long-drawn-out fighting was at its grimmest. "Tubs filled with seawater were stationed all along the ramparts, so that men burned by wildfire could immediately soak themselves. Jars of watered wine and panniers of bread were constantly ready in the main defense points, so that soldiers could get food and drink without having to leave their guard posts."

The Grand Master was harassed by another ceaseless worry. Would his urgent pleas be answered and the relief force sent from Sicily before it was too late? La Valette must have discussed this grave matter frequently with his secretary and closest confidant, Sir Oliver Starkey. All they had to go on was the vague promise from the viceroy of Sicily that help would arrive before the end of August, but the two men had little faith in his word. By early August the Turks had effectively sealed off the Knights in Malta from the outside world. Soon after this La Valette apparently gave up all hope of relief, announcing that, "there is no hope to be looked for except in the succor of Almighty God."

Nevertheless a relief force was being assembled; 8,000 men, including 200 Knights, were waiting in Sicily, with ever-growing impatience at the slowness of the viceroy to agree to their departure. The Knights, who had come hot-foot from all over Europe to help their brothers-in-arms, were particularly outspoken and restive at the petty reasons continually found for delaying their departure. Eventually, on August 25, this force set off only to be scattered a few days later by a gale. The ships had to return to Sicily to refit.

Perhaps it was just as well that La Valette knew little of these frustrating twists and turns of fortune. Though feeling abandoned by all their allies and friends, the Grand Master and his troops were determined to hold out to the end. Moreover the garrison was now deriving some encouragement from small, but unmistakable, signs that the Turks were at last losing heart. No major assaults took place during the last week of August, and, even in the great effort on September 1, the Turkish soldiers lacked their previous dash and enthusiasm. In truth, the Turks were becoming dispirited by their terrible casualties, all of which seemed so futile. Disease, especially dysentery, was rife; the wells had been contaminated before the siege began, and the full effects of this were now being experienced by the enemy. In the humid midsummer heat of the windless harbor area, the air was foul with the stench of thousands of corpses. Not only was food scarce, but so was ammunition; the prevalent sickness (accentuated by the Turkish utter ignorance of hygiene, the dead lay everywhere unburied) combined to create a sense of hopelessness, and this permeated and undermined the Turkish camp.

The morale not only of the Turkish troops but their leaders had begun to crack. This became apparent by the end of August, when Mustafa decided to try to take Medina. The capture of Malta's capital would at least be something to show against all his losses; furthermore if he did

decide to spend the winter in Malta, the control of Medina would be vital for his security. His unwilling troops set off to climb the slopes of the steep hill on which this great walled city is perched. As they approached it, they were met by cannon and musket fire. As the Turks marched around Medina, they were dismayed by the massive strength of most of its walls, which were lined by ranks of soldiers. Thoroughly disheartened they refused to consider an assault and retraced their steps. Providentially for Malta, the Turks had not seriously probed the defenses of Medina. The masses of soldiers lining the walls were only peasant men and women dressed up to play the part; the governor had had to resort to this trick to outwit the enemy, because he had so few soldiers in his garrison.

Events now began to move fast. On September 5, Balbi noted that the Turks were starting to pull out their guns and stores. Two days later the garrison saw that the Turks had withdrawn from their trenches opposite the walls. The jubilant survivors had poured out of their cramped quarters to savor to the full the freedom of being able to move around again unmolested; considerable quantities of valuable loot could also be scavenged from the deserted Turkish lines. The garrison was, however, too weak to interfere with the Turkish forces, and Balbi sadly relates how he felt sure that with 2,000 men they could have captured the Turkish artillery.

To return to the progress of the relief force. On September 4, after hemming and hawing to the last, the viceroy set sail from Sicily. His force consisted of about 8,000 men in 28 vessels, and this fleet was again partly dispersed in a storm. Although Admiral Piali had three times the number of ships under his command, he made no move to intercept the viceroy's vessels as they came by Gozo. Nor did the Turkish admiral interfere with the troops as they disembarked on beaches in northern Malta. Thus on September 7, the relief force came ashore unscathed and safely linked up with the garrison at Medina.

As soon as possible a party of Knights was assembled and rode off through the now deserted Turkish camp at the Marsa, on to Mount Sciberras, and right down to the remains of Fort St. Elmo. From the two latter vantage points they could watch the Turkish ships, laden with wounded, preparing to sail from Marsamuscetto Harbor. A hurried request was sent back for some light guns to be brought to St. Elmo to shell the vessels. In the meantime, as a final triumphant gesture, the Knights' flag, with its white cross of St. John, was run up to flutter above the ruined walls of Fort St. Elmo, a fitting memory for the Turks to take away with them.

This siege had yet another surprise in store. Once more the Grand Master had outwitted the Turkish leaders. He had released a Turkish galley slave with the exaggerated story that the relief force was 16,000 strong. As intended this information had reached Mustafa, who had believed it, but when he realized how much weaker this force really was, he flew into a violent rage. Mustafa was alarmed at the likely reaction of the Sultan—notoriously a cruel old man—at the ignominious failure of this great expedition. It might have been the last straw to have admitted to the Sultan that a greatly superior Turkish army had fled for home when faced by a mere 8,000 comparatively lightly armed men. Furthermore Mustafa now reckoned a chance existed to snatch a last-minute victory, which might save his reputation. Overriding Piali's protests (the admiral was,

as always, anxious for the safety of his fleet, and the season of autumn gales was starting), Mustafa ordered 9,000 troops to be disembarked.

Mustafa's plan was to march northwards, defeat the relief force, and re-embark at St. Paul's Bay. On learning of this reversal of Turkish plans, La Valette was wisely reluctant to give battle, since the Turks were potentially a formidable army, and he knew that no other relief force would be forthcoming if this one was smashed; furthermore, a defeat at this juncture might lead Mustafa to stay on and make another attempt at seizing Malta. There was, however, no holding the newly arrived Knights and their soldiers, who were determined to have their chance at battling the Turks. Eagerly they charged down from the ridge on which they were stationed and soon drove the Turkish soldiers back in confusion; but Mustafa rallied the rearguard, and they fought a series of bitter struggles. He distinguished himself even more than usual by a bravery that seemed to verge on the suicidal. During that afternoon he had two horses shot from under him. By evening the remnants of the Turkish army finally reached St. Paul's Bay. Here all organized resistance ceased, and a terrible slaughter began, as the tired soldiers were hacked to pieces or shot down as they struggled to reach the safety of the huge fleet, which lay offshore in the deeper water. Mustafa's last gamble had ended in a rout.

The next day the Turkish fleet set off for home. Although furious at first, the Sultan had calmed down by the time Mustafa and Piali brought their ships sadly back into Constantinople. The two Turkish leaders were pardoned, the Sultan proclaiming that he only was capable of conquering Malta.

Malta's heroic stand was applauded throughout

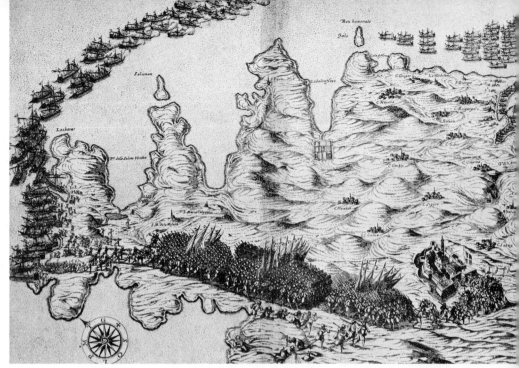

5 *The arrival of the relief force from Sicily. In right foreground stands the walled city of Medina flying the Knight's flag; the Turkish fleet is in the top right corner*

Christendom. Bells were rung in all the great cathedral towns of Europe to celebrate this first major setback to the westward expansion of the Turkish empire. La Valette welcomed the widespread publicity and interest. The conditions in Malta were dreadful. "Birgu and Senglea still smoked and disintegrated from their three months of siege. Not a single house was undamaged. . . . Hardly a man, woman, or child was unmarked by the terrible rigors of the siege. The maimed and wounded dragged themselves about their shattered fortress like figures risen from the dead." Although the relieving forces brought in supplies, it was essential to rebuild the ruined town as soon as possible. The Knights' fleet had to be re-equipped to carry on its task of harrying the Turks, and new strong fortifications were urgently needed if the island was to continue to be a bastion against Turkish imperialism. The responses to the Grand Master's appeals were generous, and money poured in from all over Europe.

Gifts and honors were showered on La Valette; but he wisely refused the Cardinal's red hat offered to him by the Pope Pius V on the grounds that his work in Malta occupied him too fully. On March 28, 1566, the foundation stone for a great fortified city was laid. It was to be built on Mount Sciberras to overlook both the Grand Harbor and Marsemuscetto. Rightly this magnificent new permanent home for the Knights was named Valetta after the Grand Master. La Valette himself died two years later, while the city was still being built. He now rests in the crypt of the majestic cathedral of St. John, and beside him lies his faithful English secretary, Sir Oliver Starkey, the only other person to be buried there.

The Siege of VIENNA
July 14—September 12, 1683

THE TURKISH siege of Vienna lasted for 60 days from July 14 to Sepember 12, 1683. The popular hero of this sensational siege was the Polish King, John Sobieski. A stout, 53-year-old warrior, he led the large cosmopolitan army that descended on the Turks to rout them just as they were going to break into Vienna. Never has a city been closer to disaster; another few hours delay would have seen the Turks pillaging and looting the capital of the Holy Roman Empire as they had done in Constantinople, the capital of the Eastern or Byzantine empire, over two centuries earlier. This conclusive defeat of the Turkish forces marked the end of their westward advance, which had been going on for more than three centuries. After 1683 the Turkish empire began to crumble, slowly at first, until it was finally destroyed, together with the Holy Roman Empire in 1918, as a result of the First World War. Thus this siege proved to be an even more decisive event in the history of Europe than had been the Great Siege of Malta, which had only halted the Turks locally.

Unfortunately, to understand the siege of Vienna, it has to be related to the extraordinarily complicated international relationships that prevailed then in Europe. Perhaps the most convenient way to set the contemporary scene is to describe first the main difficulties that faced the defenders. And after that, turn to look at the reasons why the Turks decided to attack Vienna in 1683.

Vienna was the capital of the Holy Roman Empire. With some justification it has been asserted that it was neither holy nor Roman and certainly not an empire. Certainly the Hapsburg empire, to give its accurate name, was an astoundingly ramshackle affair. The greater part of it was composed of dozens of kingdoms and principalities, scattered over what is now modern Germany. The rulers of these states owned nominal allegiance to the Emperor, but he could never rely on their wholehearted support in any crisis. The defense of the empire thus depended largely on the armed forces that could be raised and kept in being from those territories over which the Emperor had direct authority. These were Austria, Bohemia (now western Czechoslovakia), and Silesia (now part of Poland). The Emperor also ruled, or misruled, over a part of western Hungary, where border warfare with the Turkish-controlled Hungary continued endlessly.

The problem of keeping this very loosely knit Empire in existence was immensely aggravated by its having to fight on two fronts, the Turks being the enemy in the east, and the French in the west. In this period Louis XIV of France was at the height of his power. The French intrigued to the utmost against the Empire, to gain territory from it and to weaken it. Since the Hapsburg influence, however vague, was resented in many states, Louis XIV exploited these weaknesses, and, in 1683, the kingdom of Brandenburg, with its sizable army, was too friendly to France to help the Empire in this emergency. The French hostility meant also that Imperial troops had to be withdrawn and permanently detached to safeguard the western borders of the Empire. During 1682, Louis had gone so far as to urge the Turks to attack, by stressing the feebleness of the Empire and hinting that they could expect the French to intervene on their side. In fact the French did not move against the Empire during the critical summer of 1683, but the permanent French threat in the west significantly helped the Turks in the east.

In these difficult circumstances, the fortunes of the Empire were profoundly affected by two factors. The first was the need to find allies. After some hard bargaining in 1682, the Emperor's emissaries had won over Poland from the French camp. Then a powerful country, Poland was also being menaced by the Turks, and Sobieski, its King, promised to send 40,000 men to help the Empire if a crisis should occur. In return for the alliance, the Emperor promised to pay a large sum of money to the Polish King, who was always in financial difficulties.

The second vital factor, on which so much of the fate of the Empire depended, was the character of the Emperor himself. Leopold I had ascended the Imperial throne in 1657, a very young man. On the whole he proved ill-suited for this extremely arduous post, being a cautious, colorless creature who lacked the spark of leadership. For instance, he fled from Vienna before the Turks reached his capital and remained a passive spectator of the great events of 1683. Yet Leopold had one redeeming virtue, once he had chosen a subordinate he interfered little with the subordinate's conducting of affairs. In 1680, he had appointed his brother-in-law, the Duke of Lorraine, an able and experienced soldier, to command the Imperial troops. With Sobieski, Lorraine was, after some early failures, to become the other hero of the siege. The Polish King has described Lorraine. "He has an aquiline nose, almost like a parrot's; he is scarred by smallpox; he stoops. . . . His wig (a rotten one) is fair in color. His horse isn't bad, with an old saddle and trappings of worn and poor quality leather. . . . But he has the bearing not of a trader . . . but of a person of quality." Between them these two men did more than anyone else to save Vienna.

On the Turkish side, the dominant figure was Kara (meaning black) Mustafa. Grand Vizier since 1676, he was the undisputed ruler of the Turkish empire; the Sultan, Mehmed IV, normally behaved like a highly venerated puppet, spending most of his time hunting. The decision to attack Vienna was Mustafa's own, and his plan of campaign was opposed by several important military leaders, particularly the Khan of the Tartars, who commanded the largest cavalry group in the Turkish forces. Kara probably had two main reasons for wanting to capture Vienna, the first being to glorify himself by obtaining the richest prize open to the Turks. His second aim was to keep the huge armies profitably occupied outside the confines of the Turkish empire.

The Turkish advance from Belgrade began early in June. Kara had mustered a huge force, variously estimated at between 150,000 and 500,000. Although he was theoretically in command, Kara Mustafa had little operational control over the tens of thousands of Tartar and Magyar (Hungarian) cavalry who swept up the southern side of the Danube valley like some tidal wave, looting, plundering, burning, and killing everything in their path. In a disorganized fashion these irregular forces eventually pushed on up the Danube, well beyond the city of Vienna itself. Their devastation was later to cause Kara's besieging troops great inconvenience, since no supplies could be gathered from the great swath of country that they had reduced to dust and ashes. Fleeing in front of these horsemen were streams of terrified peasants trying to escape with their lives, crying, "The Turk is at the gate."

Kara Mustafa's own progress was much slower. Leading the main Turkish army, he took about four weeks to reach Vienna. It was providential that Kara moved in such a leisurely fashion, because Vienna was ill-prepared to withstand a full-scale siege. When Lorraine's forces had failed to hold the Turks on the Hungarian border, frantic and belated measures were taken to prepare Vienna for a siege, but these were started only the week before Kara Mustafa's army appeared outside the walls. On July 7 the Emperor Leopold and his court left the city, as did thousands of others, all carrying as many possessions with them as they could. The following day Lorraine entered Vienna. A determined soldier, Starhemberg, was sent to the city to command the 11,000 troops who were hurriedly put in to form a garrison. Un-

der the direction of these two able men, the fortifications were repaired and strengthened, the moat deepened, and covered ways constructed to permit the troops to get back and forth to the more forward parts of the defensive works. Cellars were requisitioned to store the gunpowder. Enough grain was brought into Vienna to last till November. Finally, on July 13, the order was given to burn down all the buildings just beyond the outer wall (known as the counterscarp); it was essential that the defenders should have an unobstructed field of fire, otherwise the Turks could have used these buildings to approach safely up to the foot of the walls. But sparks from these burning suburbs flew into Vienna, and, on the 14th, several large buildings in the city were alight; at one time it even seemed as if the arsenal, where 1,800 barrels of gunpowder were stored, might catch fire. Thus, before the wind changed and the flames moved away in another direction, the apprehensive defenders of Vienna looked out through the smoke pouring from their own city to the nearby hills, where they could see villages being burnt by the enemy.

At the very last moment Lorraine, with the cavalry, who were valueless in a siege, left Vienna and crossed to the northern bank of the Danube, destroying the bridges as he went. Vienna's defense was now solely left to Starhemberg's small garrison; Lorraine spent the next few weeks anxiously waiting nearby for the arrival of sufficient reinforcements to drive off the Turks.

Many of the outstanding events of the siege were recorded in a vivid diary kept for Kara Mustafa, the Grand Vizier. This account tells the story through contemporary Turkish eyes, and will be used extensively.

On July 13 it reports, "Half an hour before sun-

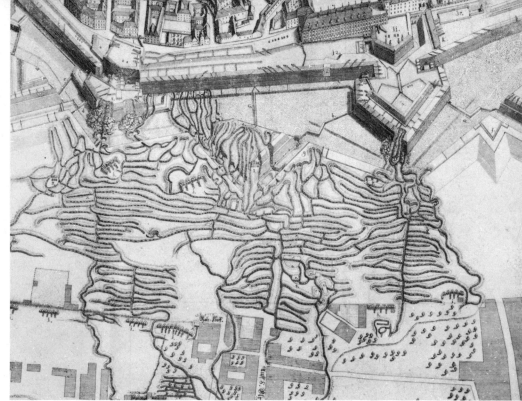

6 Detail of the Hofburg and the Turkish siegeworks, showing the complexity of the trench system at the end of the siege. Drawn by Daniel Suttinger in 1683 and reproduced from Vienna Gloriosa id est peraccurata et ordinata descripto *(Vienna 1703)*

rise the horse's tail of the Grand Vizier went off; afterwards he struck camp himself and set off for the new camp, which he reached after five hours march." Kara had a brief rest, then "he set off, with about 10,000 horsemen and no baggage, to inspect the fortress of Vienna and make himself familiar with the terrain."

Kara was greatly struck with one of the royal palaces he visited just outside the city. "It had roof covered with gilded copper instead of lead, so that when the sun shone on it one's eyes were dazzled. . . . The walls and pillars are of bright porphyry and white marble, and the garden in front of it is decked out with a great variety of flowers." The many magnificent trees impressed the Turks, who remarked especially on "the hedges of living green, which rise to a height of two lances, so

that one cannot see out from inside nor inside from without it." To crown all these delights this garden had its own zoo. So pleased was the Grand Vizier that he rested there and ordered the gardens to be well protected; a very necessary precaution since many similar places "were set alight, destroyed, or razed to the ground." Almost invariably the Turks ravaged everything in their path, being interested only in women and movable loot.

On July 14, Kara disposed his forces for the siege, giving exact details of where each commander should begin his trench system. Unlike Malta, the Turks had brought no heavy siege guns with them. Probably, based on their recent success in Crete, they had decided to rely on bringing down the fortifications by laboriously mining underneath them and not by destroying them by gunfire. To get close enough to the walls for the sappers to tunnel beneath them, communication trenches had to be dug first. In this network of trenches, foot soldiers could be stationed to storm through the breaches in the walls made after the mines were exploded. The Turkish artillery was only to provide covering fire for the attackers.

The Grand Vizier concentrated all his forces opposite the fortifications on the western side of the city, where the ground was not marshy. Here the outer suburbs were still intact, so the Turkish forces could approach unseen to within 400 yards of the outer walls of the city. On July 14, Kara's diary rejoiced that "everyone who had to enter the trench could ride his horse to the opening of the communication trenches, which were placed inside a suburb and in the middle of palaces, with gardens and pleasure houses." On that day "according to the rules of the noble Mohammedan tradition," a note was sent to Starhemberg stating bluntly, "Either Islam, or tribute—otherwise the decision in our combat will be left to the sword!

Take heed!" Starhemberg rejected the summons. The siege was on.

For the next few days the diary continued in a most cheerful vein. On July 18, it reported that "On this happy day the high-and-mighty Grand Vizier took to the trenches in the late afternoon, as the final victory seemed in sight, and decided, placing trust in God, to stay in the earthwork until . . . the fortress was captured and subdued." In fact his quarters must have been pleasant, since he lived in "a vast palace with strong walls and a courtyard in front of it, in which stand a wide variety of fruit trees."

Regarding the preparations as a whole, Kara had good cause for optimism. Although the ground was more stony than was expected, the complicated maze of deep trenches was being steadily pushed forward, and had soon reached less than 200 yards from the outer wall of Vienna. By July 17, the city was surrounded. The Turks had finally sealed the garrison off from the outside world by building two bridges over the Danube,

7 *Details of the Siege at its height. The siege-works can be seen at the top righthand corner of the city. Drawn by Daniel Suttinger in 1683 and reproduced from* Vienna Gloriosa id est peraccurata et ordinata descripto *(Vienna 1703)*

one upstream and the other downstream from the city. On this Kara "mounted his swift horse . . . and, without the slightest concern, rode around the fort within the range of a musket shot." He must have felt even more confident of rapid success when he surveyed the sprawling unprotected Turkish encampment of 25,000 tents and saw the 50,000 animals, many of them camels, which accompanied this huge army. Of Lorraine and the Imperial troops there was no visible sign; they had retired to the northwest.

During the next two weeks, however, a note of disquiet begins to creep into the diary. On July 22 the entry runs, "In this night livelier activity than previously. While the Grand Vizier was having a meal in his trench a cannon ball wounded his first food-taster in the leg." The man died of the wound. Although many mines were exploded, nowhere did the Turks make a major breakthrough. The enemy was counterattacking, and violent fighting took place on the night of July 26. On July 30, the diary records, "After afternoon prayers a mine was sprung on the right wing; it destroyed a whole crowd of the enemy, but apart from this did not achieve at all the desired effect." The following day the enemy let off a mine, but the diary claims that it did no harm "by the grace of Allah." That night "an indescribable conflict, with bombs and stones, raged for five hours," and the Turks took a palisade (a fence of strong wooden stakes). But the progress of the siege was most disappointing to the Grand Vizier. On August 2, he made a personal inspection of the forward positions. Kara Mustafa "issued severe reprimands and weighty censure to the commanders of the right and left wings, because they had not yet constructed the communication trenches satisfactorily and had shown a certain lassitude

during the day." By early August the original impetus of the attack was clearly being lost, and Turkish morale was declining.

To turn to the conditions inside Vienna during the eight weeks of siege, the most immediate danger that faced the city was destruction by fire. Most of the houses were covered with wooden roof shingles, and these were easily set alight by incendiary shells. Wisely Starhemberg ordered that roofs of all the buildings within range of the Turkish guns should be stripped; these wooden shingles, soaked in pitch, were later placed in the moat and, when set alight, illuminated it against the Turkish night attack. An acute shortage of heavy timber for defensive works soon developed, but this was overcome by removing the heavy timbers from buildings already without roof coverings. By the end of the siege the many roofless houses gave the city a strange, derelict look.

Bombs and shells exploding on hard, stone surfaces cause much greater casualties and damage than those landing on soft earth. Starhemberg, like Eliott in Gibraltar a century later, commanded that all the paving and cobblestones be dug up from the streets. Like the timber and roof shingles, these stones were all put to good use; some were piled up to form barricades against enemy fire, some were used as ammunition by being dropped on the enemy storming the walls, while the large paving stones were invaluable in repairing the damage to parts of the fortifications.

Inevitably the authorities were confronted with many unexpected social problems. Housing was one of the most immediate of these, since thousands of refugees from the surrounding countryside, fleeing before the Turks, had poured into Vienna. At first they just camped in the streets

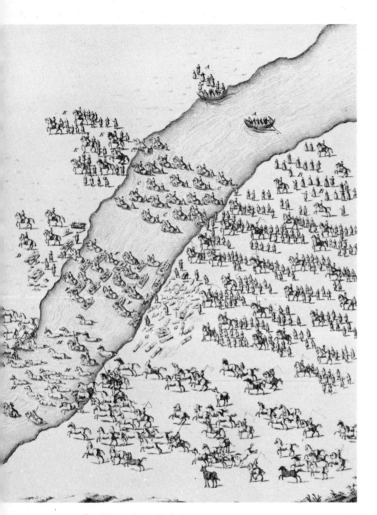

8 *Tartars and their prisoners crossing a river. From L. F. Marsigli,* L'état militaire de l'empire Ottoman, ses progrès et sa décadence *(The Hague 1732)*

A and B *Women captives*
C and E *Prisoners tied to tails of horses*
D and F *Rafts of reeds used to ferry stores across the river*
G *Bundles of reeds*
H *Captured horses*

and must have been very vulnerable to enemy gunfire. But many families had left the city, and their empty houses were soon taken over by the homeless.

Another much more unpleasant obstruction began to clutter up the streets; refuse of all kinds, including people and horses killed by enemy shot and shell, accumulated everywhere. Rubbish disposal presented an almost impossible problem; dumping into the Danube had to be stopped because the river was so low that it did not wash the garbage away. Fearing a terrible epidemic, the town councillors, the mayor, and doctors laid down directions that the blood and refuse from freshly slaughtered animals should not be thrown into the streets and that all dirt and rubbish should be removed from the streets, since, at a council meeting, it was asserted that an epidemic was caused by the filthy streets "in which soldiers and poor sick people lie bleeding, over whom other people have to step." To improve matters a little, the leatherworkers were mobilized to skin the carcasses of rotting oxen that had been cast into the streets. Large pits were dug, but very soon overflowed with rubbish. In the end even the drains and sewers were stuffed full of the mounting quantities of rubbish. The hot weather added to the stench, and, when Vienna was relieved, it was remarked that the atmosphere was poisonous. Being beside the sea both Malta and Gibraltar escaped the worst of this refuse hazard and its effects on health, while Paris had the advantage of a more sophisticated refuse-disposal system as well as the Seine flowing through the city. In addition, the siege of that city took place mainly in the winter months.

In a cramped and crowded city that is being besieged, finding space to bury the dead soon becomes a terrible problem. The death rate in Vienna on August 13 was thirty per day, two weeks later it had doubled. As early as July 29 all the normal burial grounds were full. The authorities then took over some of the monastic cemeteries, but by the middle of August these were inadequate, and mass graves had to be dug in various gardens.

Vienna was grievously and increasingly afflicted by a prolonged outbreak of dysentery, which probably caused more casualties than the Turks. Besides the hygienic precautions already mentioned, the authorities issued three other decrees, vainly trying to reduce the prevalence of this disease. First they ordered that the black bread eaten by the army should be thoroughly baked to render it more digestible. Secondly they forbade the selling of freshly brewed warm beer, which had not properly fermented. Finally army wives were ordered not to buy herrings; it was discovered that salted, pickled, and smoked meat and fish, especially herrings, were being washed down with liberal quantities of sour wine, which resulted in stomach troubles. In spite of these sensible efforts, it proved impossible to check the dysentery that seriously weakened the strength of the garrison; even Starhemberg himself fell a victim to it, while the mayor almost certainly died of dysentery in September. To make matters worse, the hospital arrangements were, at first, very rudimentary. An energetic bishop did all he could to improve things by turning the monastic houses into hospitals. He spent considerable sums of money procuring help, food, and equipment for the sick and wounded; but one of the gravest shortages was straw, which meant that many had to go without even the comfort of straw mattresses and had to lie on the bare earth or the floor. By the end of August, the city was in a desperate situation, with all the hospitals overflowing and medical supplies almost exhausted.

During the first few weeks of the siege, food was fairly plentiful, and prices were effectively controlled, especially for dried goods like rice, lentils, and wheat. But the livestock was quickly slaughtered, and fresh meat soon became so scarce and expensive that cats were sold as "roof hares." Starhemberg confiscated cattle that had somehow been smuggled in with the connivance of the Turks. He also got the town council to put a stop to women climbing over the walls to exchange bread for fruit and vegetables with the Turks; the nature of the "appeal" to these citizens was stressed by erecting three gallows in a prominent position! By early August, however, prices were rising steeply, and shopkeepers had to be threatened with the confiscation of their stocks if they sold above the permitted maximum prices. As always in sieges, the bakers were the most troublesome group of tradesmen. The quality of the bread soon deteriorated; this was partly because there were not enough flour mills to grind the wheat finely and partly because there were insufficient ovens to bake the quantities of bread needed. More ovens were built, but, nevertheless, several decrees had to be passed to try to check bakers from profiteering. From August 13 each baker had to put his personal mark on all the loaves he baked, and supervisors tested the weight and quality; at the end of the month bakers were forbidden to sell better quality white bread secretly at great profit. In spite of all these measures, food prices began to reach fantastic heights early in September and, to make matters worse, the grain and the pickled meats were all beginning to go rotten.

There may be a tendency to distort an account of any siege by overemphasizing the miseries that had to be endured. The greatest distress probably occurs at the beginning of many sieges, when people are unaccustomed to the hardships, and again at the very end of the siege, when the besieged are at the end of their physical and moral tether. Certainly in Vienna, the first week strained everyone's nerves. A nun wrote, "There has been such a bombardment by day and night, that we have not known where to go, we have been so shocked and frightened. At first we hardly went to bed, we were so fearful." Within a week the tension had relaxed, the ordinary people were sleeping at night, and many pursued their normal occupations. The churches were packed. On July 24, during a sermon in the great church of St. Stephen, a cannon ball came through the roof and landed in the organ pipes, but little damage was done to the church. About ten days later the roof of another big church collapsed on to the congregation, who rushed out, but a contemporary remarked that they "soon returned and did not let anything turn them from their worship."

Certainly those locked up in Vienna had good reason to pray endlessly and devoutly that they would not be handed over to the mercy of the Turks. The diary of the Grand Vizier cheerfully tells how those in one small town accepted an offer of surrender in return for a promise to be spared. When "they were completely unarmed, the Turkish raiders suddenly shouted the Muslim battle cry, drew their sabers, and mowed a number of them down. They then swarmed into the town from all sides, where they raped the boys and girls, pillaged all articles of any value." The account concludes rather smugly, "This, too, is a sign of the grace of Allah, who had so deranged

the wits of the enemy that they could not keep their heads in such a situation."

The siege had now developed into a grim slogging match. The Turks were slowly and relentlessly breaking into Vienna by tunneling underneath the defenses and then blowing them down. But it was a costly and lengthy process to destroy the three strong bastion walls and cross the two moats against such determined opposition. Almost daily Mustafa's diary reported events such as, "After sunset a mine was sprung, which knocked down a good section of the pigsty of the infidels." The diary also frequently recorded the valiant sorties of the garrison, as on September 1 when "the infidels carried out an attack . . . for half an hour there raged a conflict of such bitterness that it defies description."

Nevertheless, by the beginning of September, the Turks were within measurable distance of victory. But their heavy losses had begun to affect their morale, as incidents like this showed, "Four men were caught drinking wine against the infidel's palisade; each of them was publicly given 200 strokes." Food was running short, and no fodder could be found for the animals, so that "it was necessary to journey for three or four days to get hay." Kara's temper was getting very uncertain, as was demonstrated when he "flew into a mighty rage, grabbed him [a Pasha] in a fury by his beard and showed his skill at distributing boxes on the ear." The victim was boxed over the ears again for refusing to remove his "robe of honor." Kara must have also been aware that many of the Turkish leaders had already collected large quantities of booty and only wanted to return home to enjoy it.

While Kara was beset by mounting problems outside the walls, inside Vienna itself Starhemberg was almost overcome by the multitude of difficulties he had to face. His gravest problem was the physical condition of the garrison. On September 4, a huge mine exploded and weakened the garrison, who were only just able to repulse the subsequent Turkish onslaught. A few days later it was estimated that sickness and battle casualties had reduced the garrison to 4,000 men, out of the original 11,000. An equally intractable problem was the exhaustion of those still fit to fight; the soldiers had been in action almost continuously for over seven weeks and could not go on for much longer. About 5,000 civilians were organized into formations, and helped in guard duties, but were unwilling to perform the more hazardous tasks of repairing the damaged fortifications. By September Starhemberg had conscripted many of them and forced them to give more effective assistance.

Starhemberg had one consolation. By the early part of August it was obvious to him that the Turks had committed, for some unexplained reason, all their forces against the two great bastions on the western wall of Vienna. Hence Starhemberg could safely concentrate all his resources on defending this one sector of the city. His small garrison could hardly have held out against attacks from several different quarters.

The spotlight must now be switched to the armies that were converging to relieve Vienna. In the first place, Lorraine had kept his small army of 10,000 intact, and he used this to check the Tartar raids and thereby keep the route open for the Polish forces advancing from the northeast. He also positioned his force as close to the city as he could. Intermittently, Lorraine received messages from Starhemberg; these were carried through the Turkish lines by volunteers, who were paid a high price for their dangerous missions. Lorraine also sent messages back into Vienna, promising relief by early September and urging the garrison to hold out till then. The safe arrival of these messages was signaled by rockets fired from the city and by smoke from Lorraine's army, which could be seen by now, in the distance across the Danube, from the tower of St. Stephen's Cathedral.

The most important contingent in the relieving army was provided by Sobieski. His journey from Poland to Austria was an agonizingly slow affair. He set out from Warsaw on July 18, and ten days later reached Kracow, where he spent nearly four weeks. Sobieski's slowness can be partly explained by the unusually early start of the campaigning season; the Turks did not normally begin their land wars until August or early September, and, therefore, the scattered Polish troops were not prepared for battle and took some time to assemble. By mid-August Lorraine was sending urgent requests to Sobieski, stressing the critical state of the garrison. By the end of August, Sobieski had arrived near the Danube, and Lorraine met him. The Polish King had brought about 20,000 troops. About the same time John George, the Elector of Saxony, had completed his journey from Dresden and entered Austria with over 10,000 troops. The third important force consisted of 10,000 Bavarian and Franconian troops, under Maximilian II Emmanuel, the Elector of Bavaria.

With so many illustrious rulers congregated together, the command of the armies could have been a cause for much wrangling. Fortunately the hesitant emperor was not a serious candidate and thus Sobieski was the natural choice. Happily he agreed with Lorraine's plan that the assembled army should cross the Danube by bridges that

Lorraine had had built about 15 miles upstream from Vienna. Once across the river, there came a difficult operation, since the army had to advance through the hilly and heavily wooded Wiener Wald before it could take Kara's forces in the rear.

By September 6 the combined armies of 60,000 men had crossed the Danube unopposed. The three following days were spent in forming up, prior to the final two-day approach march through the difficult Wiener Wald region.

Though Kara knew the route of the relieving army, he did surprisingly little to try to check its advance or to fortify his camp against attack from the rear. At a conference it was agreed that the siege should continue and that the Turkish cavalry should fend off the "infidel army." On September 10, the gravity of the situation became clearer when twenty German prisoners were taken and, in the words of the diary, "19 of these were put to the sword and one was sent to the Grand Vizier for a friendly chat." During this "friendly chat," the prisoner convinced Kara that 100,000 troops were descending on him. That night he ordered a general alert, but nothing happened except that the garrison let off large numbers of rockets to emphasize their plight. Encouraged by this, Kara pressed on with the siege. On September 11, final preparations were completed to blow up the remaining defenses, and it must have seemed to Kara that Vienna was as good as captured.

September 12 was the fateful day. Very early that morning Kara's diary reckoned that "200,000 of the accursed infidels were in sight" and, it continued, "it was as if a waste of black pitch flowed down the mountainside, which crushes and burns up everything that withstands it." All that very hot morning, Kara's 28,500 troops, mainly composed of horsemen, grappled with Sobieski's army as it emerged from the hills and woods at the back of Vienna. During the early afternoon there was a pause in the fighting, as the allied forces regrouped. At 3:20 P.M. Sobieski's army attacked in full strength; two hours later the outnumbered Turks broke and fled.

According to his diary, Kara "was determined to find death on the battlefield." He was, however, dissuaded and escaped, together with the famous "Flag of the Prophets," which the Christians had hoped to seize. Even Kara's influence could not long withstand such a disaster. On Christmas Day he was stripped of all his powers and ceremoniously strangled; so ended the rule of the last of the all-powerful Grand Viziers.

As for Sobieski, he entered Vienna in triumph and, having given thanks in church for the victory, he went to a banquet given by Starhemberg the next day in the devastated city. Lorraine refused to attend—he was too angry at the delay; all he wanted to do was to pursue the disorganized Turkish forces. On September 14, the Emperor Leopold returned to his capital, from which he had so hurriedly departed nine weeks earlier. Quarreling soon broke out among the allies about future plans. Nevertheless Vienna had been saved just in time, by an almost miraculous combination of outside forces. Christendom was secure thereafter from the Turkish threat. For the Turks this was, in the words of one of their eminent historians, "the most important campaign in their history."

The Great Siege of GIBRALTAR
1779-1783

GIBRALTAR IS one of the few places that fully lives up to its reputation. It looks every inch a fortress. Magnificent, dramatic, yet rather sinister, this massive hunk of rock rises out of the surrounding sea like some huge, stranded whale. From whatever direction it is approached, Gibraltar dominates its surroundings.

Its importance has always been recognized, being occupied in turn by the Phoenicians and the Carthaginians before the Romans seized it. In 711 the Moors besieged and retained it till 1309, when it was conquered by Spanish forces. For the next 200 years Gibraltar underwent eleven sieges! For the following two centuries the Rock led a remarkably peaceful existence. Until, in 1704, the British, under Admiral Rooke, took it after a very brief siege, only to be themselves besieged directly afterwards. In 1727 the Spaniards made another unsuccessful attempt to recapture Gibraltar.

A glance at a map brings out Gibraltar's strategic importance. In much the same way as Malta controls the central Mediterranean, so the Rock of Gibraltar dominates the western end of this almost landlocked sea. At the Straits of Gibraltar the great landmasses of Europe and Africa almost meet each other, with the Rock situated less than twelve miles from the North African shores. Thus all vessels wishing to pass in and out of the western end of the Mediterranean have to run the gauntlet of the ships and guns stationed at the Rock.

Physically, Gibraltar is a tiny place, a mere 2¼ square miles in extent. It is a startling, precipitous, narrow strip of land, running north and south for less than three miles. The north face is most dramatic and formidable. Here the Rock rises almost vertically for 1,200 feet, to soar above the thin, low-lying spit of land that connects it to Spain like a sort of umbilical cord. For nearly two miles the top of the Rock consists of a knife-edged, spiny ridge that reaches a maximum height of 1,400 feet at Sugar Loaf Point. From here the ground falls away sharply, and the southern end of Gibraltar is composed of two plateaus, the smaller and lower of these is about 50 feet above the sea and is called Europa Flats. On its eastern flank, Gibraltar is most imposing; almost

9 Plan of the Bay, Rock, and Town of Gibraltar, from an actual survey by an officer who was at Gibraltar from 1769 to 1775, with the works, batteries, and encampment of the Spanish army on October 19, 1782, and the position of the combined fleet and the attack by the battering ships, September 13, 1782. Engraved by William Faden

everywhere the ground plunges down into the sea in a series of precipices. Only on the western side are there relatively gentle slopes, and along the water's edge, there are some pieces of flat land. Most of Gibraltar's buildings are clustered on the west and look across the magnificent great semicircular Bay of Algeciras, which is everywhere backed by distant peaks.

In spite of its great natural strength, Gibraltar as a fortress has some serious drawbacks. No good fresh water springs exist, and nearly all the water supply has to be caught; rain in the summer is very rare. Though often delightful, the weather in Gibraltar is sometimes trying. The Levanter, an unpleasant easterly wind, brings a stream of muggy air that soon makes everyone irritable and, for days on end, can shroud the upper heights of the Rock in clouds. From time to time sea mists occur that blot out the Straits. As in Malta, the summer heat can be exhausting, and the discomfort used to be accentuated by an extreme shortage of water, which increased the problems of health and hygiene. But perhaps Gibraltar's gravest weakness is its dependence on the outside world for food. So barren is its surface that virtually no crops, except a few vegetables, can be grown. Nevertheless the Great Siege, which lasted almost four years, triumphantly showed how, with the aid of sea power, a resolute garrison led by a determined commander can surmount these handicaps.

The immediate cause of the Great Siege was that Spain had made common cause with France in the American Revolution. Earlier in this war the British had fared so badly in America that France had decided to take advantage of this and had joined with the colonists in 1778. By exploiting British difficulties in America, the French hoped to recover most of the overseas possessions they had lost to Britain during the Seven Years War of 1756–63. Always ready to seize on a chance of recapturing Gibraltar, Spain in 1779 had joined her ally France. Opposed by the joint forces of France and Spain, Britain was then fighting most of the Western world single-handed. This war benefited none of the participants except the American colonists, who gained their independence.

In 1779 the main fighting strength of the garrison was the five British infantry regiments stationed there. These consisted of the 12th (Suffolk), 39th (Dorset), 56th (Essex), 58th (Northampton), and the newly formed Manchester Volunteers, which were disbanded soon after the siege; these first four regiments still proudly have as their crest the Castle and Key of Gibraltar, and below this are written the words of the motto of the Rock, *Montis Insignia Calpe*, the "Badge

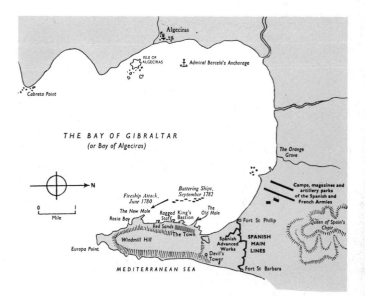

10 Simplified map

of the Mountain Calpe," Calpe being the old name of Gibraltar. In the garrison there were also three much smaller Hanoverian infantry regiments, as well as about 500 gunners and 120 engineers. This force numbered about 5,380 men. The direct dependents of these troops numbered some 1,500 women and children. A census in 1777 estimated the civilian population at 3,200, composed of 520 British subjects, 860 Jews, and the rest mainly Portuguese and Spaniards. Finally, under the naval commander Admiral Duff, were five vessels, the sixty-gun *Panther*, the twenty-eight-gun *Enterprise* and three smaller ships whose crews totalled 760. Thus in round figures, about 10,700 people were locked up in Gibraltar when the siege began.

Perhaps the most outstanding thing about the siege was the personality of its governor,

Lieutenant-General George Augustus Eliott, the younger son of a Roxburghshire family of some influence. In 1777, at the age of 60, this teetotal, vegetarian widower had been appointed governor. He had spent over 40 years in the army and had campaigned with increasing success all over the world. He was furthermore a dedicated and professional soldier, having studied military engineering as well as learning to speak fluent French and German. A recent biographer summed him up in these words, "he never slept more than four hours at a time. A stern but just disciplinarian, he was a man indifferent to the niceties of military parade and etiquette . . . he was often spoken of with deep respect, even veneration, as far as his military qualities were concerned. . . . Eliott inspired confidence, with little cordiality or personal devotion." His appointment was a stroke of genius.

In the two years before the siege began, Eliott exerted his considerable influence with the government at home, as well as employing his energies, drive, and skilled knowledge to the improvement of the defenses of the Rock. He continually pressed for more troops, but the garrison never reached 8,000 men, which he considered to be the number needed. Eliott stockpiled supplies of all sorts. He obtained more artillery; indeed, by the end of the siege, Gibraltar had accumulated the impressive total of 663 serviceable guns, mortars, and howitzers.

Eliott also devoted his efforts to improving the fortifications of the Rock itself. Here he was exceedingly fortunate to find in Colonel Green a brilliant senior engineer officer who had been working on this problem for over 12 years. During this period Green had transformed many of the fortifications and had constructed the King's bastion, a powerful defensive position covering a vital stretch of the western side of the waterfront. On the potentially vulnerable northern side, the defenses had also been strengthened. The only road into the Rock from Spain led along a narrow causeway skirting a triangular flooded area (the Inundation). A ditch with a drawbridge was the next obstacle that had to be negotiated before reaching the entrance gate. This was guarded by a tunnel (Landport), through which the road twisted before finally emerging into Gibraltar itself. The whole approach area was covered by the fire of dozens of guns, well concealed and protected in lines on the hillside above. Parapets and covered ways led to these batteries, so that the gunners had the maximum protection from enemy fire. Throughout the siege, working parties were continuously improving and strengthening the existing strongpoints as well as building new ones. It was thus small wonder that the Spanish troops had little enthusiasm for direct assault on a place so bristling with guns and other fortifications.

This siege began very quietly. On June 21 no mail arrived from Spain. British officers going out riding into Spain for their morning exercise were turned back. Eliott received a polite letter from the Spanish commander stating that he had orders to cut off Gibraltar. A month later the Rock was under close blockade. The Spanish had clearly decided to try to starve the British out. Eliott put the garrison on a warlike footing. Fresh water was rationed, all stray dogs were killed, as were horses not needed for essential purposes or whose owners could not show they had 1,000 pounds of feed in hand for each horse. The summer passed by uneventfully, and a few ships slipped in from Morocco with stores and left crammed with civilians wanting to escape. Prices had risen steeply by

September, and luxuries such as a duck cost 7s (shillings), or twelve dollars today.

Early in the morning of Sunday, September 12, 1779, the peace of the Bay of Algeciras was shattered. The British batteries on the North Face fired into the Spanish lines. Tradition has it that the young wife of an artillery officer lit the taper that fired the first shot; two days later Eliott forbade soldiers' wives "to go up the hill on account of their irregular behavior." The Spanish did not retaliate; indeed Eliott's reason for opening fire was primarily to improve the morale of the garrison, who were becoming depressed by the dreariness and hardship of the blockade.

As autumn turned into winter, the blockade was felt more and more harshly. Few ships managed to pass through the Spanish fleet patroling off the entrance to the Bay of Algeciras. The shopkeepers were profiteering heavily, releasing very meager supplies, and continually increasing their prices. The soldiers were not as badly off as the civilians. They were paid 4½d (pence) per day (corporals, 6d, and sergeants, 9d) and received a weekly ration that consisted of:

7 lbs bread
2½ lbs salt beef
1 lb salt pork
10 ozs butter
½ gallon pease (dried peas)
3 pints groats (crushed grain, usually oats)

This allowance was increased for those of higher ranks. Thus warrant officers and lieutenants were issued with two and majors four of these rations; the abstemious Eliott had 24 rations. A contemporary account given in Captain Drinkwater's diary, makes gloomy reading, "The bakers had long been limited to the quantity of bread issued to the inhabitants, and sentries were placed at the wickets, where it was delivered to prevent confusion and riot. . . . A soldier, his wife, and 3 children would inevitably have starved to death, had not the generous contribution of his corps relieved his family . . . thistles, dandelions, and wild leeks were for some time, the daily nourishment of numbers."

The plight of those locked up in Gibraltar was made worse by the shortage of fuel, always a major problem in any lengthy siege. Two godsends, however, occurred. After a very severe storm after Christmas, quantities of wood were washed ashore. Two weeks later a merchant ship was forced into Gibraltar carrying 6,000 bushels of barley. Nevertheless, early in 1780, General Eliott concluded a dispatch to the government in these words, "no supplies—our provisions daily consuming—many inhabitants near starving." There were signs that discipline was beginning to crack. A soldier was hanged for stealing, the first execution of the siege. Several soldiers tried to desert and fell to their death. Strangely some Spanish troops tried to reach Gibraltar. The hardships in the Spanish camps, where the trenches were flooded, were almost as bad as those in Gibraltar, and fever was rife and food scarce.

Suddenly the exhilarating rumor went around that the British fleet was approaching. On January 10, General Eliott cut the soldiers' rations, but even this did not dampen the general optimism. On January 15, the first British vessel came into sight and cleverly eluded the waiting Spanish warships. The whole garrison and all the civilians seemed to be crowded around the New Mole to welcome in the brig *Sophia* and her crew. To add to the rejoicings, the price of flour plummeted from 2s to 6d a pound. The shopkeepers took alarm that they might be left with unsold supplies, and suddenly all manner of goods previously unobtainable were displayed in shop windows.

For the next few days nearly everyone spent their time watching for the fleet. More and more British vessels sailed into Gibraltar, bringing with them tales of Rodney's successful battle against the Spanish fleet off Cape St. Vincent. Rodney himself did not arrive until January 26, being on board his 90-gun flagship HMS *Sandwich*; but even this magnificent ship was overshadowed by the *Royal George*, which carried 100 guns. Among those serving in it was the 15-year-old midshipman Prince Wiliam Henry, third son of George II (later to become William IV), who was shown around the Rock by Colonel Green. Of equal interest to the garrison was the wounded Spanish Admiral Juan de Langara, captured when the 80-gun Spanish *Phoenix* had been taken; he was put ashore at Gibraltar. The supply ships of Rodney's fleet had restocked Gibraltar with essential stores, except spirits and soldiers' uniforms. To strengthen the fortifications further, some heavy guns were put ashore from the captured Spanish vessels. But even more important, Eliott was able to reinforce substantially the garrison. He retained in Gibraltar the 2nd Battalion of the 73rd Regiment (now the Highland Light Infantry), which had originally been destined for Port Mahon in Minorca, where the Spanish were also besieging the British. In addition, 2,000 sailors remained in the ships that stayed on at the Rock after the main fleet had sailed.

On February 13, 1780, most of Rodney's great fleet left for England. The garrison watched them go sadly, but some spectators had a particularly personal concern for the safety of these ships.

Eliott had rightly ordered that all "useless mouths" should be evacuated, and many soldiers had to be parted from their wives and children. In spite of this evacuation, 2,500 civilians still remained in Gibraltar.

With the departure of Rodney this prolonged siege entered into its second phase. The naval blockade was resumed and intensified, and the garrison soon found itself back on the same monotonous rations, though these were larger than before the relief. The staple foodstuffs had been augmented by a big consignment of salt Newfoundland cod, acquired by Eliott from one of the merchant ships. Never a popular dish, this hated cod stank abominably by the summer. But much more serious, many of the provisions that had been landed were maggoty and moldy and deteriorated rapidly in the hot weather. To introduce some variety into the diet, Eliott instructed those with gardens to grow vegetables and sell their surplus. Somewhat surprisingly the commercial vegetable gardens in the neutral zone, between the Rock and the Spanish lines, were still unmolested by the enemy, who permitted the owners to tend their crops. Also some fishing was carried on by local boats. Occasionally a small ship from the outside world would sneak in to sell its cargo of live meat, chickens, fruit, and wine at a handsome profit; these luxuries were beyond the reach of the ordinary soldiers and the majority of civilians. In the evening the wine shops would open, many selling a vicious concoction of wines called blackstrap. Since no other entertainment existed for the soldiers when off duty, these drinking dens were well patronized.

One effect of the siege was to increase the numbers of children. A soldier wrote, "we marry and breed faster than ever known in peaceable times." Naturally, on such a poor diet, the children were especially susceptible to disease. An epidemic of smallpox lasted from February until August and killed about 400 children. The mothers were particularly incensed with Eliott, since he refused to permit the crude form of inoculation that then existed. Cut off as they were from fresh fruit and vegetables, scurvy proved a terrible trial; by September Gibraltar was suffering widely from this complaint, which shows itself in spongy gums, bad-smelling breath, spots, aching limbs, and general lassitude. Thus the three great trials of siege warfare, hunger, disease, and boredom, severely afflicted those locked up in the rock during these long months.

During the very dark night of June 6 the routine of the garrison was suddenly shattered. The Spanish secretly approached the New Mole, where nearly all the British shipping was concentrated, out of range of enemy shore-based guns. Approaching to within a few hundred yards of the coast, the Spanish ignited and set loose nine large fireships. Though taken completely by surprise, the naval crews reacted extremely quickly. Some put out in small boats, carrying grappling hooks, others directed well-aimed shots and thereby diverted these dangerous craft from their objectives. If the fireships had set ablaze the British vessels, the devastation could have been catastrophic, since many of them had been prepared for the voyage back to England and had dozens of barrels of gunpowder stored between decks. If they had caught fire, the blaze would almost certainly have spread to the great stores and magazines kept on and near the New Mole. Anticipating this chaos, the Spanish fleet stayed waiting to pounce on and destroy any ships that tried to escape to sea. And if the Spanish plan had

succeeded, their warships would probably have closed in to bombard the stricken area. Luckily the wind soon dropped and caused the current to drift the ships away from the threatened foreshore. Several of their charred remains ran aground at Europa Point, where they were quickly broken up for fuel. In the midst of all the night's uproar a boat from Tangier entered Gibraltar unharmed.

Although understandably shaken by this attack, its utter failure boosted the garrison's self-confidence. But, as the exceptionally hot summer of 1780 wore on, conditions inside Gibraltar slowly but steadily deteriorated. Yet despite the intense strain nobody talked of surrender. Any slackness was mercilessly punished, and a soldier was given 500 lashes for being asleep at his post.

In October crackers replaced bread. Money was almost worthless. Mrs. Green refused £60 for a small cow. The shopkeepers became less and less prepared to sell their hoarded goods, and by February, 1781 the bakers had ceased to work. The Spanish had now sealed off Gibraltar so effectively that very few ships managed to run the blockade. The Sultan of Morocco also turned against the British and forbade ships to sail from Tangier to Gibraltar; he imprisoned and then expeled the British Consul, who had done such invaluable work organizing supplies from Africa. Other sources of food were also cut off. The Spanish no longer permitted the cultivation of the gardens between the lines, while the fishermen were attacked so consistently that they gave up trying to go to sea. To relieve the gloom a passing vessel was captured and found to be carrying oranges and lemons. This windfall of fruit brought the scurvy epidemic under control, and Eliott preserved the rest of this precious cargo by mixing the fruit juice with brandy. Almost certainly this prize of oranges and lemons saved the garrison from capitulation by disease.

The opening months of 1781 were perhaps the blackest of the whole siege. Sheer boredom coupled with inactivity and hunger were having a serious effect on morale. Rations were cut. Cracker dust cost 1s per pound and a bottle of beer 2s 1d. Desertions became more frequent although only 43 were recorded during the whole siege. Two men were hung for robbery. Officers presented lists of complaints to Eliott; they were embittered at the lack of promotion, since casualties were very light. Yet Eliott carried on grimly, keeping the garrison as busy as possible. Regiments were paraded for field days. New tunnels were dug high up in the north face of the Rock, overlooking the Spanish lines. New types of artillery were devised, including mortars carved out of solid rock. The gunners were kept fully occupied firing at the Spanish. And always, Eliott was steadily strengthening the fortifications. This task daily employed most of the men in various parts of the Rock.

At long last conditions improved dramatically. As the fog slowly cleared on April 12, the garrison and the townspeople flocked to the water's edge, cheering with joy to behold what an eyewitness described as "one of the most beautiful and pleasing scenes it is possible to describe." Anchored in the Straits lay 29 great ships-of-the-line, and clustered around them were about 100 merchantmen. As the supply ships moved toward Gibraltar they were attacked by gunboats, but the escorting naval vessels easily drove them off. Several fled to the nearest shore, where their crews abandoned ship. Unfortunately the Navy so despised these "bum boats" that they did not

bother to destroy them, and thus these annoying little ships were later refloated to resume their bombardment of the Rock.

This was to be a day of incredible contrast, since, just as the relief ships safely reached the quays, the delight of the onlookers was turned to panic, and with very good reason. The long-awaited Spanish bombardment had begun. The concentrated fire of 114 heavy guns and mortars was directed on to the town and waterfront of Gibraltar. Shots and shells exploded among the assembled throng, who fled southwards in pandemonium to the security of Windmill Flats and Europa Point. This intensive barrage continued for about two hours, then from 1 P.M. to 5 P.M. it stopped as suddenly as it had begun, siesta time had arrived. The Spanish resumed their fire from 5 P.M. onward, a regular procedure during the next few months. On April 13 alone about 3,000 shots were fired into Gibraltar, and the town was soon reduced to a shambles. The partly demolished houses revealed all sorts of hidden stores. The temptation to loot proved too much for the soldiers. Many of them ran riot looting the hoarded liquor, food, and goods that the rapacious merchants had kept concealed, hoping to make even greater profits. For nearly two days the town was given over to scavenging soldiers. In this prolonged drinking bout unconscious soldiers perished in the shelling, while others drank themselves to death. Order was only restored when the sober Hanoverian regiments took over and flushed the drunken soldiers from their hiding-places.

All this time the great naval relief force lay out at sea. It was commanded by Admiral Darby, who never personally visited Gibraltar, but sensibly kept his ships in the tranquillity of the Straits.

Although an undistinguished figure, Darby was cooperative, handing over to Eliott as much gunpowder as he could spare from his vessels. By this generous act, 2,280 barrels reached the Rock, thus enabling Eliott's guns to return fire freely.

Throughout the bombardment the job of unloading went on. So speedily did the men work that the unloading was almost completed in a week, and, despite the enemy's heavy fire, casualties were surprisingly few. On April 20, Admiral Darby decided to sail for England, and about 1,000 civilians took passage with the fleet; 141 of them, being captured en route by the Spanish, were sent back to Gibraltar! Thirteen coal miners had not yet been unloaded and were sunk off the New Mole, and their cargo removed in a more leisurely fashion. Some further supplies arrived later, and with these vessels came Captain Curtis, who stayed to command the naval side of the garrison and soon made a name for himself second only to General Eliott.

After this restocking of Gibraltar, another phase in the siege began. Having failed to starve the garrison into submission, the Spaniards now substituted a new policy of 'round-the-clock bombardments to batter those on the Rock into surrendering. By day, except for siesta time, the guns and mortars on the isthmus hammered away at the town and its defenses, and about 77,000 rounds were fired in seven weeks. By night the attack was taken up by gunboats. Rowed close into the shore, they fired their single large guns into those areas out of range for the land-based guns. The almost continuous Spanish fire in no way disheartened the defenders, whose casualties were light. The British guns and mortars retaliated vigorously, so the Bay of Algeciras ceaselessly resounded to the boom of gunfire, while the spring air became acrid with clouds of gunpowder smoke.

In the town itself, the plundering and looting was stamped out after several soldiers were hanged and others given hundreds of lashes. Rough punishment was also meted out to three soldiers' wives who had been found guilty of receiving stolen goods (some soap). They were stripped to the waist, the hangman gave them a dozen lashes on the bare back with a cat-o'-nine-tails, and they had labels stating their crime pinned to their breast.

During the roasting summer of 1781, the monotonous routine of siege life was resumed, but the enemy shelling slackened off somewhat by early June. Most of the men's spare time was spent in trying to improve the flimsy new living quarters that had been run up in the southern tip of the Rock, beyond the range of the land-based guns.

By the autumn, scurvy again seriously afflicted the garrison, who were saved only by the arrival of four small fruit boats. But Eliott and his men had by now another and more pressing problem. There was unmistakable evidence that the unwilling Spanish commander, Alvarez, had been prodded by Madrid into making an assault. From their bird's-eye-view at the top of the Rock, the British could observe the Spanish lines stretched out far below them, where it was becoming more and more evident that the enemy was pushing its trench system toward the British outposts. Several new Spanish gun positions were being built, and a high parapet wall constructed to mask these preparations. Late in October, Eliott agreed that the gunners should put down a concentrated barrage to try to knock down this parapet wall. It lasted most of one night, but it had little effect, since the Spanish used the sand of the isthmus to rebuild the shattered parts of the wall. In this emergency the defenders were spared one great anxiety because they knew tunneling to be impossible in the low-lying isthmus, where any trench dug deeper than four feet deep reached the water level. All the Spanish preparations had to be above ground and thus could be easily seen.

During most of November Eliott himself was hardly ever visible. He even ceased his normal nightly rounds of the garrison posts on his white pony with its muffled hoofs. In the utmost secrecy, he was conferring with a few chosen advisers and planning a daring sortie against the Spaniards. The first the garrison knew of this was after nightfall on November 26. That evening the wine shops were shut. "Evening Garrison Orders" appeared giving detailed instructions for those involved; the password was "Denbigh" and the countersign, "Steady."

For this sortie Eliott assembled a force of over 2,000 men. Divided into three columns, the whole of the 12th and Harderberg's Hanoverian regiments provided the main body, being reinforced by all the grenadiers and light infantry from the other regiments. With each column went detachments of gunners and engineers, and a party of Curtis's sailors was included. The plan was to level as much of the enemy works as possible, to spike their guns and to destroy their gun positions and magazines. This was to be accomplished by the gunners and engineers while the infantry protected them. The gun batteries on the Rock were to provide covering fire.

From interrogating experienced observers and from his own long and careful observation, Eliott had been able to gain a detailed knowledge of the Spanish dispositions. He reckoned that his opposite number, Alvarez, would never believe that the tiny garrison could, or would, risk a sortie. Eliott was aware that the majority of the 15,000 Spanish troops opposing Gibraltar were encamped by night too far behind the isthmus to intervene rapidly; furthermore he was convinced that the enemy positions were not easily defensible. Nevertheless, even with seasoned troops, a sortie on this scale was an extremely daring act, but one that could result in worthwhile damage to the enemy's schemes. On the other hand, Eliott's personal appearance among the forward troops that night can only be called a foolhardy performance, though it was fully in keeping with the old man's character. A terse conversation has been recorded between Brigadier Ross, the commander of the forces, and Eliott.

ELIOTT: *"What do you think of the business? Is it not something extraordinary that we have gained the enemy's works so easily?"*

ROSS: *"The most extraordinary thing is to see you here!"*

The sortie proved remarkably successful. The Spanish opposition was negligible, their forward works ruined, their guns spiked, their magazines blown up, and their wooden structures left blazing. All this was accomplished in about 2 hours, with British losses at 4 killed and 25 wounded; 2 officers and 16 other ranks were brought back prisoners from the 78 Spanish who manned these forward lines. The morale of the garrison was immensely improved by this display of strength and determination. Eliott's dispatches home naturally made the most of this outstanding event. Besides pleading for more men, he forwarded a long list of supplies he needed, including camphor, cream of tartar, emetics, 24 scalpels, a dozen bone nippers, and 4 dozen stump pillows. One of the prisoners had to have his leg amputated and, though well cared for, died. A solemn truce was arranged for; the body was sent back by sea with full military honors. The fate of this young man had moved the garrison deeply, because he had been engaged to a beautiful Spanish girl who had sent him gifts of food and clothing while he lay desperately ill. It was typical of Eliott that all the delicacies not consumed were returned with his corpse!

The beginning of 1782 is a convenient point to take stock of the general situation. Scurvy and boredom were perhaps the two major problems, but occasional incidents reduced the tedium. Especially exciting were the grandstand views of ships trying to elude the blockade to reach Gibraltar. The spectacle of Spanish vessels endeavoring to capture blockade-runners filled the watchers with agonizing suspense; groans would greet the failure that led to capture, while cheers echoed out for the successful ship as it entered Gibraltar.

Yet the daily routine must have become terribly dreary, particularly the monotony of the food. It resembled the hard tack issued to sailors at sea, only unlike most voyages, this one had now lasted almost continuously for two and a half years. During the latter stages of this siege, the shortage of liquor must have been a penance for hardbitten older soldiers, who were so accustomed to heavy drinking. Furthermore living conditions were ghastly, with the bulk of the garrison still existing in makeshift huts or tents on the southern end of the Rock. In the winter these provided little protection against the cold and wet, in the summer they gave only nominal shelter against the heat. These quarters were also liable to be hit at night by shells from Spanish gunboats; early in June, the British sailors were equipped with 12 gunboats to counter these attacks, which they did with increasing efficiency. No regular news came from home, and, as no proper postal service existed, the married soldiers could never rely on hearing from their families back in England. The toughness of the veterans of the Rock garrison can be judged by the early performance of the reinforcement regiment. The 97th had arrived on March 21. Sickness hit them so hard that within three months about 100 had died and so many of them were in the hospital that they only produced their first picket of 40 men on June 17.

Two outside events occurred that were to have important consequences for Gibraltar. The first was the British surrender in October 1781 at Yorktown. This virtually ended the war in America, and the French could therefore put all their resources into helping Spain. In February 1782, the second blow fell when Minorca had to capitulate, and this released about 12,000 seasoned French and Spanish soldiers, many of whom were soon to be employed against the Rock. These disasters did, however, have one important side effect for Gibraltar. They concentrated attention on the heroic stand of the garrison there, so that it became a symbol of British pride. Popular demand clamored for more help to be sent to the Rock and belatedly forced the feeble government of Shelburne to take action.

Throughout the oppressive summer of 1782, tremendous preparations were proceeding for a decisive assault on the Rock. Reinforcements poured in. On May 26, the Bay of Algeciras came alive with sails, when a fleet of over 100 ships entered its sheltered waters. The observers on top of Gibraltar estimated that about 9,000 troops disembarked, which brought the assembled Franco-

11 Floating batteries. Detail from an engraving by Bergmiller

Spanish force to over 31,000. Great camps constantly sprang up around the shores and foothills of the northern end of the Bay of Algeciras.

Across the bay, the garrison could also watch the progress in converting ten large galleons into floating batteries. These complicated ships were the invention of a French engineer called D'Arcon. By strengthening the sides of these vessels and by covering them with a very thick layer of fireproof material into which rows of water pipes were laid, D'Arcon reckoned that they would be impregnable to all types of shot. In his view, they could be brought close inshore to bombard Gi-

braltar's defenses with their heavy guns, and a way would therefore be opened to land troops from the sea. After this the enemy's plans became rather confused. But it was suggested that once the floating batteries had done their task, the combined fleets of Spain and France would put the troops ashore, and simultaneously the land armies would storm in from the isthmus to capture Gibraltar.

Although outwardly the enemy was supremely confident, heated arguments went on among its commanders. Most of the trouble centered around the elderly Duke de Crillon, who had just arrived from Minorca to command the forces attacking Gibraltar. As an experienced soldier, the duke realized well the risks of a landward attack against so powerful a fortress. On the other hand, he resented the publicity and influence that D'Arcon had already acquired for his scheme and feared that if the young Frenchman's invention succeeded, all credit for the victory would go to him. As the summer went on relations between these two men became very strained, D'Arcon becoming more and more exasperated when the conversion of the galleons into battering ships was hindered by unforeseen technical difficulties and by the dilatoriness of the Spanish workmen. So jealousies and delays disrupted the enemy's plans.

The increased rate of desertions and an outbreak of dueling showed that the morale of the garrison was affected by the evidence that the enemy was massing his forces. Hardly any ships managed to creep into Gibraltar, though on May 3 supply ships unloaded 1,900 barrels of powder. Later that month about 80 Corsican refugees arrived. They proved a loyal, though quarrelsome, contingent, and Eliott wisely quartered them on Windmill Hill, the highest place on the Rock. Even at this critical time, Eliott received little encouragement from home. He was, however, heartened by Rodney's victory over the French fleet in the West Indies and he ordered a salute of guns to be fired, which, as he had intended, annoyed the enemy.

Two events broke the monotony and tension. The first nearly resulted in a disaster. A 13-inch shell penetrated a magazine in one of the positions facing the isthmus and blew up 100 barrels of gunpowder. Drinkwater relates that, "The explosion was so violent as to shake the whole Rock and throw materials on both sides an almost incredible way into the sea." Fortunately it did not set off the neighboring magazines, nor were the Spanish guns able to do any further damage. Fourteen men were killed and 15 injured in this explosion, but the damage was soon repaired.

The second event was also heralded by an "explosion that was so amazingly loud that almost the whole of the enemy's camp turned out at the report. But what must their surprise have been when they observed from whence the smoke issued." It was from a small hole high up on the north face of the Rock. After two months tunneling through the soft rock, Sergeant Major Ince and his men had made a passage along which guns were soon brought. From this dizzy height cannons could fire into almost every part of the Spanish lines. Sergeant Major Ince's work has been carried on ever since, until today the rock is a maze of underground tunnels.

By the beginning of September, 80,000 spectators had flocked in to enjoy the thrill of seeing Britain kicked out of her last foothold in Europe, a pageant to be performed in the magnificent setting of the Bay of Algeciras. In the great camps were quartered 40,000 troops, clad in the gorgeous uniforms of the eighteenth century, particularly colorful were the horsemen of the Spanish cavalry regiments. One of the biggest forces ever assembled for any siege was here and one of the most discontented. This spectacle reached its visual climax on September 12, when new flotillas of French and Spanish warships sailed in Algeciras Bay; 500 vessels of all sorts were now anchored in the bay and these included 3 three-deckers, the largest warships in the world; 40 other ships of the line, 90 smaller naval vessels and several hundred transports; 6 admiral flags could be discerned in this forest of masts. During September

1782 probably more sailing vessels were gathered together on this one small piece of water than have ever been assembled before or since.

This apparently ill-matched struggle had in fact begun four days earlier. Surprisingly the opening move had been made by Eliott and his little garrison of 7,000 weary men. Early on September 8, 60 heavy British guns started a 9-hour bombardment on a new sand-banked wall 1,000 yards away from the Rock. By evening 5,500 shots had been fired. The secret British weapon had done its work, for the guns had been firing red-hot cannon balls, which took 3 hours to heat and an hour to cool, and these, lodged in the woodwork of the wall, soon started fires that became too numerous to control. Round one had been won by the British. Eliott had seized the initiative.

This unexpectedly fierce British barrage infuriated Crillon, who felt himself publicly humiliated before the eyes of the vast concourse of distinguished spectators who had assembled expecting an easy triumph. He decided on immediate retaliation. At 5:30 A.M. on September 9 he ordered all the land-based guns to open up against Gibraltar. Thus once again the dawn was heralded by the roar of gunfire, which sent the apes scampering up the Rock to take shelter in caves. The speed and weight of this bombardment surprised Eliott's men, since they had not imagined that the Spanish positions could be repaired so soon. At first some losses were caused by a newly prepared 64-gun battery that enfiladed many of the bastions on the north front, but the British soldiers were so experienced in siege warfare that they soon found cover. With the continuous noise of 170 guns firing, with reverberations of this gunfire resounding from the Rock, with a dozen or more shells in the air at the same time and each one trailing behind it a tail of smoke, the watchers who crammed every vantagepoint must have felt that their journey had been worthwhile. Nevertheless, though 5,403 rounds were fired, Drinkwater drily remarked that "their effects were not equal to the numbers expended."

As if to complete the spectators' highest expectations, later that day some Spanish and French warships joined in the action. As they sailed proudly along, parallel with the waterfront, they fired broadsides. At Europa Point they turned about and repeated their performance. This bombardment did little material damage. It delighted the Gibraltar gunners, giving them a welcome opportunity to let fly at the passing vessels and "return their salute." This piece of naval showmanship proved a blessing to the garrison, who collected the numerous 26-pound cannon balls that lay scattered around. Hundreds of these were soon to be heated up and fired back at the enemy from their own guns; along the seaward defenses the crafty Eliott had installed all the 26-pound guns removed from captured Spanish ships!

As the sun began to set, 15 Spanish gunboats were seen to be approaching Gibraltar. There was enough daylight left for the garrison to do some accurate shooting, and several boats were hit before they could withdraw. The enemy fire now slackened off, but all through the night shells burst over the Rock among the working parties repairing the damage and carrying up ammunition to restock the gun positions.

For the garrison, the night of September 9 was a sleepless and nerve-racking one. Since he expected the attacks to be renewed next day, Eliott ordered the grates to be lit and cannon balls heated. He was determined to use these "hot potatoes" against any ships that dared come within range. On September 10, Admiral Moreno's fleet sailed out again to "shoot up" the Rock. This time the sea walls were lined with the troops who, ignoring the danger, were determined to view the fight. As the warships went by firing, each battery opened up in turn with their red-hot cannon balls. Unlike the day before, the enemy ships did not venture a return journey, but headed for home to the accompaniment of mocking cheers from the garrison. At least one "hot potato" had found its mark, and the Spanish decided to abandon this hazardous and unrewarding maneuver.

All day the bombardment from the isthmus continued. Eliott did not retaliate. He was saving his fire for the climax of the siege. Everyone was waiting for the attack by the battering ships. Eliott had made all possible preparations, including building more grates for heating up the cannon balls.

On the enemy's side, Crillon was in a fury. Admiral Moreno was equally angry. Only too obviously their plans had, so far, failed. Now D'Arcon and his floating batteries had to save the day. Spanish pride could not permit any more delays, especially after the grand fleets of Spain and France had finally assembled on September 12. Crillon ordered D'Arcon to attack the next day. He overruled the Frenchman's protests that his vessels were not ready and that the water depths had not been properly charted where the vessels were to be anchored. The attack was to be on Friday, September 13, come what may, and Crillon refused to listen to any excuses.

That night, September 12, unhappy D'Arcon went out in a small rowing boat to take soundings off the Gibraltar waterfront. He was horrified to discover a large sandbank about a thousand yards from the Old Mole, just where he intended to

anchor some of the battering ships, and, on his return, was further dismayed to learn that Admiral Moreno had given orders that the ships should be manned, which meant that there was no possibility of briefing each captain. In addition D'Arcon was deeply perturbed because he had been given no chance to test the ships under practical conditions.

With a northwesterly breeze blowing, the weather on Friday was perfect for this operation. At 7 A.M. the 10 top-heavy ships clumsily set sail, looking something like Chinese junks or floating haystacks. Five of these floating batteries were fairly small, with a crew of about 350 men, and each carrying on the average 9 large cannons. The 5 bigger ships carried a total of some 3,500 men, and mounted altogether 110 guns, with a further 70 in reserve.

It took about three hours of complicated maneuvering for this flotilla to reach its moorings. But by 10 A.M. the line of battering ships was anchored in apparently perfect position off Gibraltar, and the cannonade began. Immediately the Spanish and French guns on the isthmus also joined in, so that, together with the guns of the garrison, some 400 pieces of heavy artillery were firing almost simultaneously. Huge crowds of soldiers and civilians, as well as the sailors on the hundreds of ships that crowded the harbor, watched entranced.

Having anticipated that the battering ships would be brought into position under the cover of darkness, Eliott had not ordered the grates to be lit that night. Thus for the first two hours, the British were sending cold shot against the assault ships, which had little effect other than bringing down their rigging; also many of the guns that were firing from the north front batteries were out of range, and their shots fell into the sea. The four battering ships at the northern end of the line were also firing mainly into the water; due to a list, their guns could not be elevated sufficiently to hit the shore, and the sandbank opposite the Old Mole prevented them coming any closer in. Another battering ship was behind two of the other vessels and so could not fire her guns. The main struggle, therefore, developed into a duel between the British gunners around the King's Bastion promontory and the two biggest battering ships, the *Pastora* and the *Talla Piedra*, which were anchored about 800 yards offshore. Being moored close to each other, they could concentrate their 47 guns on the defenders. The *Pastora* flew Admiral Moreno's flag, and he commanded her personally, while D'Arcon himself was aboard the *Talla Piedra*, as was the Prince of Nassau.

By midday smoke was hanging so thickly about the waterfront that it was hard to see what was happening. Yet the garrison never let up for an instant. The conditions for the Spaniards imprisoned between the low decks of the two largest battering ships were horrible. The smoke-laden air was suffocatingly hot, the decks were slippery with the blood of the dead and wounded, whose cries and groans could plainly be heard in between the roar of the guns, and the ships themselves were being continuously and ominously jarred by the stream of cannon balls that had found their mark. With great bravery the crews sought to remove the red "hot potatoes" that hit the ships. At about 2 P.M. the gunners on the King's Bastion saw smoke issuing from the *Talla Piedra* and redoubled their efforts. Soon the crew realized that their ship was aflame. Frenzied searches unearthed the cannon ball, but the inrush of air sent the smoldering timbers up in flames too strong to be extinguished.

By the end of the afternoon the guns of the doomed *Talla Piedra* had ceased firing, and the *Pastora* was burning too. On the isthmus the Spanish and French guns had already stopped firing, their ammunition being exhausted. Thus by about 8 P.M. the only guns still firing were the British ones. Eliott now relieved the weary artillery men, replacing them by a detachment of naval gunners, and these continued the job of destroying the helpless enemy ships. As the day drew to a close, it was obvious that the garrison had successfully repulsed the attack by the battering ships.

For the Spanish, the terrible question arose concerning the fate of their vessels, for, with masts and sails shot away, the battering ships were immobilized. Not wishing to risk his fleet in a rescue attempt, the Spanish commander decided to blow up all the battering ships by exploding their unexpended supplies of gunpowder, even if it meant sacrificing the men still on board. At midnight some Spanish boats did creep in to try to take off the crews of the condemned ships. In the fiery darkness, the British sent shot and shell into them; some were hit, while others fled before taking off all the crews.

In the early hours of September 14, Captain Curtis, the British naval commander, set out to rescue the trapped and stranded men, but as daylight came he was forced to stop his work of mercy. It had become too dangerous; first one vessel blew up with a tremendous explosion, and soon afterwards another one went up as its powder barrels exploded. To add to these hazards, the guns on the isthmus opened up again, and shells landed among those who had been rescued and were being brought ashore. Throughout the morning of September 14, other ships blew up, and through the smoke the watchers could sometimes observe men desperately climbing aloft, while others threw themselves into the sea—very few of those on the battering ships seemed able to swim. The Spanish Admiral Morena had taken no risks, but had got away from the *Pastora* early the previous evening. D'Arcon had escaped too, but he had gone back for help, bravely returning to the *Pastora* before finally reaching safety.

It had been an overwhelming victory. The enemy had lost all its battering ships, which had done little serious damage to the defenses of Gibraltar. Of the original 5,000 who had set out, 1,500 men had been killed and 350 prisoners had been captured. The garrison had only lost 16 killed and 68 wounded. Among the trophies they had acquired was a very large Royal Ensign of Spain, which had been carried on the *Pastora* in anticipation of its being flown from the highest point on the Rock!

In retrospect, the most remarkable thing about this whole battle was the passiveness of the combined fleets and armies. Throughout September 13, hundreds of warships lay motionless and 40,000 armed men made no move against the garrison. The defenders of Gibraltar were thus able to concentrate their efforts on destroying the two battering ships that had managed to bring effective fire to bear on a small part of Gibraltar. If, as Eliott had feared, a properly coordinated attack had been mounted, the garrison's resources would certainly have been critically dispersed. But Crillon hated D'Arcon so much that he refused to help him; while Admiral Moreno was so angered by the insults Crillon had hurled at him about the feebleness of the naval attacks earlier in the month, that he did not order the fleet out in support of the battering ships.

The 80,000 spectators had witnessed an almost incredible fiasco, 7,000 men had repulsed 60,000

to the accompaniment of 40,000 rounds of ammunition being discharged. The British alone used up 716 barrels of gunpowder for the 8,300 shots they fired, half of these being the red-hot cannon balls.

The remainder of this siege now appears as an anticlimax. But this was not how it seemed to Eliott and his hard-pressed men. The tension was kept up. On September 14 a large contingent of French and Spanish troops marched from their camps down to the isthmus; while in the Bay of Algeciras, some of the vessels seemed to be preparing for an assault. Nothing, however, came of these warlike preparations. Crillon had obviously lost his nerve, but he kept up a very steady bombardment.

By the end of September, life had returned to normal. The garrison had, however, found a new and profitable pastime in fishing out floatsam and jetsam; rich hauls were to be had from those wrecked battering ships whose magazines had not blown them to bits. All kinds of treasures were retrieved, some were gruesome objects like decomposed bodies, others were of more practical value, like candles, linen, and great quantities of timber. Eliott had a fine set of tables fashioned from salvaged cedar, filling up the holes made by fire with sound wood. This furniture is still at the Convent, the governor's official residence.

During the night of October 10, a hurricane hit the Bay of Algeciras. It tore many ships from their moorings, including a fine new Spanish two-decker of 72 guns, called the *St. Michael*; 634 prisoners were taken off this ship, which was worth £14,000. Several other disabled vessels were also driven close to Gibraltar, but, to the sorrow of the garrison, the French and Spanish got them back to safety when the storm had blown itself out.

From the prisoners taken off the *St. Michael*, the garrison first learned that a relief force under Admiral Howe was approaching the Straits. This apparent good news did, in fact, depress the authorities in Gibraltar, since they realized that Howe's fleet would be seriously outnumbered by the combined fleets of Spain and France. But Howe skillfully avoided battle with the superior enemy fleet. He landed two infantry regiments and a considerable amount of warlike stores, but, strangely enough, no food, so that the garrison continued to subsist largely on the provisions brought in during the second relief, over 18 months previously. A few merchant ships' captains profiteered disgracefully by selling some goods at wildly inflated prices. Eliott took the opportunity to send Captain Curtis back with Howe's fleet. Curtis made the voyage home to Britain in *Victory*, later to be Nelson's flagship at Trafalgar. Thus the third relief of Gibraltar took place successfully during mid-October 1782. But peace was still some way off.

Throughout the late autumn and winter the siege dragged on. With plentiful supplies (Howe had brought an extra 1,500 barrels of gunpowder), the garrison kept up a good rate of fire on the diminishing number of enemy. The monotony was broken by quarrels among the members of the garrison; by combating the antics of the Spanish, who were vainly hoping to blow up the Rock by driving a tunnel inside it; by the arrival of an occasional blockade-runner carrying fresh supplies of food; and, most unexpectedly, by the appearance, just before Christmas, of 150 women. They were wives of men in the two regiments that Howe had landed; they had been traveling in a different ship from their husbands, and it had been captured by the Spanish. Together with their baggage, they were ceremoniously exchanged, at an agreed rate, for the Spanish crew of *St. Michael*. Seventeen of these women were kept in the hospital when it was found that they had venereal disease, a sickness from which Gibraltar was then quite free. Unfortunately this quarantine

12 The North Front of Gibraltar, as seen from the Spanish lines during the land and sea attacks, September 13, 1782. From an engraving by T. Malton, after G. F. Koehler

was broken disgracefully, because, after a New Year's party, a group of drunken officers broke into their ward and "attacked" them.

On January 29, 1783, a final bombardment was made by Spanish gunboats. On February 2 the garrison heard the cry *"Todos amigos."* This exclamation of friendship was confirmed on February 5, when Crillon officially informed Eliott that the blockade was ended. In a masterly piece of understatement, Drinkwater wrote, "This return of tranquility, this prospect of plenty and relief from the daily vexations of so tedious a siege, could not fail to diffuse a general joy throughout the garrison." One immediate result of the ending of the siege was a fairly widespread halving of prices.

The siege ended, the eighteenth-century courtesies of war were duly performed. The Duke de Crillon sent his formidable opponent a gray horse. Soon afterwards Eliott and some of his senior officers were shown around the Spanish lines, dining at San Rocque with the duke on March 30. The following day the duke visited the Rock and inspected the defenses, which greatly impressed him, as did the youthfulness of the garrison, who were turned out to greet him during his tour. The day almost ended in disaster, when the duke's horse shied as a 17-gun salute was being fired to speed him home after dinner. The old man, however, just saved himself from being unseated.

For the garrison, the grand celebrations took place on St. George's Day (April 23), with a series of 21-gun salutes and a parade at which the official letters of thanks to the garrison were read. Processions followed, the massed bands played "God Save the King," Eliott was invested with the Order of the Bath, and 160 cannons were fired off. The garrison then settled down to the serious business of eating and drinking; all the other ranks were given 1 pound of fresh beef and a quart of wine each, while Eliott, with the senior members of the garrison and their staffs, sat down to a banquet at the Convent. Only two things marred the festivities; first, nothing was provided for the angry junior officers, and secondly the weather was wet.

In this siege of nearly four years, the British casualties were: 333 killed or dead of wounds, 1,034 dead of disease (over half of scurvy), 138 disabled, and 43 deserted. For children and civilians the deaths must have approached 1,000, since 500 succumbed to the smallpox epidemic in 1780. The financial rewards of war were a most important aspect of any campaign and these were partially distributed during 1784, but more bounty money came in later. Out of the total, Eliott received £3,375, a pension of £1,500 per year, and in 1787 was made Lord Heathfield. The private soldiers each received £2 12s 4d, sergeants over twice that sum, captains about £75, and so on up the scale of rank, with the lieutenant-governor (Boyd) receiving half Eliott's bounty; rank was most important, hence the frustration in the garrison at the lack of promotion during most of the siege.

After the siege, Eliott stayed on as governor. Unfortunately, age did not mellow him. He indulged in several private disputes with local Gibraltarians, and, more justifiably, with the home government for being so slow in clearing the harbor of wrecks. He returned to England in 1787 to receive his belated barony, and died three years later in Germany as he was setting out to return to Gibraltar.

Epilogue

The story of the Siege of Gibraltar quickly made a wide appeal to all lovers of adventure. The famous Baron Munchhausen claimed that he came to the Rock in Rodney's fleet and stayed to help his old friend Eliott. One exploit will show the ingenuity of this eighteenth-century superman. He borrowed a 48-pounder gun and waited until, through his telescope, he saw the enemy about to fire a 36-pounder. "At that very instant I gave the signal for our gun to be fired also. About midway between the two pieces of cannon, the balls struck each other with amazing force, and the effect was astonishing! The enemy's ball recoiled back with such violence as to kill the man who had discharged it by carrying his head fairly off, with sixteen others that it met in its progress to the Barbary Coast, where it passed through three masts of vessels that then lay in a line behind each other in the harbor." His own cannon ball "dismounted the very piece of cannon that had just been employed against us and forced it into the hold of the ship, where it fell with so much force as to break its way through the bottom. The ship immediately filled and sank, with above a thousand Spanish sailors on board, besides a considerable number of soldiers." Of course the British gunner, without first telling the baron, had put a double charge of powder in the gun!

The Siege of PARIS
1870-1871

FRENCH HISTORY has often been marked by violent contrasts, and never were these reversals of fortune more dramatically demonstrated than between 1867 and 1871.

In 1867 Napoleon III's 15-year-old Second Empire seemed to be brilliantly secure and universally accepted. The Great Exhibition of Paris opened punctually. Set out in pavilions in the park of the Champs de Mars (where the Eiffel Tower now stands), this glittering display of the scientific and artistic wonders of the world attracted many eminent rulers in a Europe still plentifully supplied with crowned heads of state. Among the visiting royalty, all dressed in the most glamorous uniforms, was the gay Prince of Wales, with his kind but insignificant wife; the Tsar and Tsarina of all the Russias honored the exhibition by their presence, as did the King of Prussia, accompanied by Bismarck. To see the products of nineteenth-century progress also came the Sultan of Turkey, while from Japan, the Mikado (the Emperor) sent his brother. The French Emperor, and Eugenie, his Empress, entertained their distinguished guests with a succession of magnificent balls and at special performances at the opera.

In addition, hundreds of thousands of less illustrious visitors crammed themselves into Paris to see the sights. The shopkeepers, the restaurant proprietors, the hoteliers, as well as the pickpockets and prostitutes of this magnificent but dissolute city, all reaped a rich financial harvest. The impecunious students, however, protested bitterly at being ejected from their attics to make way for more prosperous tenants, and the poor people also found that prices rose everywhere.

At the time of the Great Paris Exhibition the world appeared to be in a peaceful state. Yet a mere three years later, in July 1870, France and Prussia were on such bad terms that Louis Napoleon declared war on the Prussians. Bismarck was delighted. Partly by means of the famous Ems telegram, he had cleverly maneuvered the French into becoming the aggressors in this conflict. Fairly universally disliked, the French had tarnished their image by the arrogant manner in which they continually boasted of the efficiency of their own armed forces, and by their scornful attitude toward the Prussian army. As soon as war began, however, the chaotic condition of the French armed forces rapidly became evident. Instead of the French invading Germany, as they had intended, by September 1 a well-organized Prussian army had completely routed one of the two main French armies. Napoleon III himself had to surrender to the Prussians. His regime disintegrated, and the Empress Eugenie managed to escape with difficulty from Paris to England, where she was later joined by her sick husband. (In the crypt of Farnborough Abbey lie three enormous marble tombs, wherein repose the bodies of Napoleon III, his Empress, and their only son, who was killed fighting for the British against the Zulus in South Africa. The last French imperial dynasty eventually came to rest in Hampshire.)

The immediate political effect of Napoleon III's downfall was the creation of the Third Republic in Paris. Formed under conditions of mass emotion, this government was largely composed of lawyers, the two leading members being Favre, the Minister of War, and Gambetta, the Minister of the Interior. The governor of Paris, General Trochu, somewhat unwillingly accepted the appointment of president and commander of the armed forces. Most of the volatile inhabitants of Paris were delirious with joy at the ending of the unpopular Second Empire, and seemed certain that somehow the Prussians would soon be driven out of France. It was to be like 1792 all over again, when the newly aroused French people, having overthrown the monarchy, gained a most unexpected and decisive victory over the invading Prussian army at Valmy. On September 5, the return of the exiled poet and novelist Victor Hugo threw the Parisians into raptures of enthusiasm,

and he wrote a grandiloquent document called *Appeal to the Germans*. It lauded Paris as "the city of cities . . . in which the beating heart of Europe is felt." Victor Hugo continued, "Is the nineteenth century to witness the dreadful sight of a nation fallen from civilization to barbarism abolishing the city of nations—Germany extinguishing Paris?"

On September 13, Paris experienced another wave of exhilaration, enthusiasm, and mass confidence when a huge march past of soldiers was staged. The diarist Goncourt recalled how tremendous cries of "*Vive La France! Vive La Republique! Vive Trochu!*" arose as that general and his escort galloped by. Then the seemingly endless parade began, to the accompaniment of the "Marseillaise" being sung quietly. Even the usually skeptical Goncourt was stirred by this demonstration of the faith in France and by the way in which all ranks of society were marching united in a common cause. He felt that this display of popular determination might even result in a military miracle, by which France would be saved. On the other hand, General Trochu's original feeling of pessimism was intensified by the obviously raw and untrained condition of most of the soldiers who had filed past him.

During the first half of September, two Prussian armies pushed steadily on toward Paris. Even in the annals of military history, their 150-mile march was a remarkably bibulous affair, since, as a contemporary reported, it was marked by "two almost continuous lines of broken bottles all the way from Sedan." After a minor engagement outside Paris at Chatillon, the Prussian armies invested the city on September 20. For the next 130 days Paris was to be besieged.

September 20, 1870, is a convenient date to take stock of the general situation. After their astonishingly complete victory over the French armies, the Prussians rapidly readjusted their plans. Rightly they decided that Paris must be taken if France was to be effectively defeated. To invest the French capital, however, the Prussians had available less than 150,000 men, and Moltke, their commander-in-chief, had no intention of launching a headlong attack with such a small force. Instead he methodically began to occupy and fortify the more important positions around Paris. In this task he was helped by the flight of most of the local inhabitants, which enabled his men to take over almost empty villages and turn them into strong points. Originally Moltke's main fear was that a powerful contingent of Trochu's half million soldiers might launch a sudden counterattack, since the Prussians could only hold the perimeter of Paris very lightly with an average of one soldier per yard. On the basis of optimistic intelligence reports, however, Moltke expected that Paris would capitulate within 10 weeks.

Around some outposts of the beleaguered city, both sides often coexisted peacefully. Professor Michael Howard has described how "German sentries watched benevolently as Frenchwomen scoured the fields for potatoes; working arrangements were made for the alternate use of inns and baker's shops lying between the two positions, and a direct traffic grew up between the two armies, winked at by the German general staff, whereby German sentries traded their rations for information, brandy, and newspapers. For official parleying or the transmission of communications by neutral powers, a post was established at Sèvres. There the bugles on either side of the river would sound a ceasefire. Then, for a mere parley, the officers concerned would clamber over the barricades at either end of the bridge and converse across the gap blown in the middle. For more extended negotiations, or for the conveyance of neutrals into or out of the city, a boat was provided by the French."

As the Prussians approached Paris, Favre, the War Minister, tried to negotiate an honorable peace with Bismarck. The Frenchman hoped that the new regime might obtain reasonably liberal terms from the victors, whose quarrel had been primarily with the defunct Second Empire. But when the two men met, on September 19, the Iron Chancellor contemptuously refused to accept anything less than the whole province of Alsace and most of Lorraine, as well as the immediate surrender of the towns of Strasbourg and Toul, which were still holding out. These demands were far too harsh for Favre to accept. The newly formed republic was thus committed to a war to the bitter end with the confident and triumphant Prussians.

As the Franco-Prussian War moved into its second stage, prospects of France being victorious were very faint. If the Prussians were to be forced to withdraw from their soil, the French would have to exert a combination of three powerful influences on their enemy. First, France would rapidly have to raise and equip large armies in those provinces as yet unoccupied by the Prussians; confronted with this kind of military threat to their security, it was just conceivable that the Prussians might lose confidence and negotiate a settlement. Secondly, world opinion would have to be swung over to support the French cause wholeheartedly, and thus lead to the Great Powers applying pressure on Prussia to make her offer peace terms acceptable to France. Thirdly, Paris would have to hold out long enough to enable the other two influences to become effective.

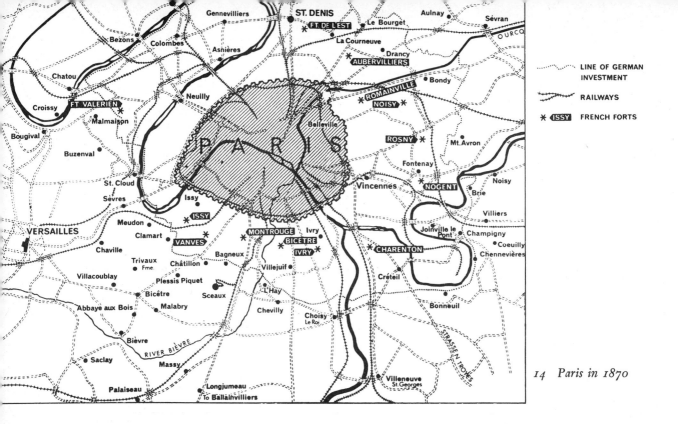

Legend on map:

.... LINE OF GERMAN INVESTMENT

〰〰 RAILWAYS

✳ **ISSY** FRENCH FORTS

14 Paris in 1870

In some ways Paris was immensely strong, having been designed as a fortress. It was surrounded by a wall 30 feet high, divided into 93 bastions linked by plain walls. A moat 10 feet wide ran in front of this long wall, while behind it was a railway for bringing up troops and supplies to the ramparts. Beyond the moat, at distances of 1 to 3 miles, lay a chain of 16 powerful forts, each of which had between 50 and 70 heavy guns. Stretching for a circumference of nearly 90 miles, all of these forts were sited to be within artillery range of their immediate neighbors.

Nevertheless these impressive fortifications suffered from grave weaknesses. In the 30 years since they had been built, heavy guns had been developed that could severely damage the walls and even some of the forts themselves. Furthermore, in some places the fortifications were overlooked by heights outside the city walls, and from these vantage points the enemy could shell the defenders with the modern long-range guns, some of which had actually been exhibited by Krupps at the Paris Exhibition. Parts of the walls had also not been properly maintained, but this was to some extent remedied by the intensive building of earthworks in the weaker places and by the laying of electrically fired landmines. Frivolous Parisians enjoyed spending autumn Sunday afternoons watching these activities.

By the end of September, Paris was full of troops. About half a million were under arms, including 75,000 regular soldiers, most of whom had failed to reach the battle of Sedan and had straggled back to Paris. There were 13,000 naval veterans, who manned many of the guns; 100,000 young territorials called "Mobiles" had been brought into the city, many of these Bretons who spoke no French. The largest force, however, consisted of the National Guard, 350,000 having been recruited inside Paris; paid one and one-half francs per day, they lived at home and elected their own officers. Although the untrained National Guard were full of bravado, they were almost useless against the professional Prussian soldiers. To make matters worse many National Guard battalions felt little loyalty to the government in Paris and were led by officers with extreme left-wing political views. General Trochu thus commanded a very mixed bag of troops and, moreover, lacking confidence in their fighting efficiency, he was understandably disinclined to risk any kind of offensive action.

With about 3,000 guns of various calibers, Paris was well supplied with artillery. Most of the heavier weapons were in static positions, but there was also sufficient mobile field artillery for French needs, and factories were soon producing more guns and ammunition. In the more obvious ways Paris went about preparing for her ordeal with efficiency and speed; even the prostitutes were herded into workshops to make uniforms, while many public buildings were requisitioned for warlike purposes.

At first the food stocks looked inexhaustible. In particular, the quantity of live meat impressed all observers: 250,000 sheep and 40,000 oxen were said to be pastured in the famous Bois de Boulogne park, and everywhere livestock were to be seen grazing on other green spaces in the city. Unfortunately, the energetic Minister of Commerce had not arranged for cows to be sent into Paris, and the shortage of milk later severely affected the health of young children. Cartloads of vegetables poured into the city that September. Enough grain and flour had been stored to last for an estimated 80 days of siege; the coal supplies were on a similar basis. Apparently this enormous inrush of food lulled most people into a false sense of security, and few bothered to lay in private stocks while this was still possible. At the time, it was not appreciated that the population of Paris had increased by about half a million to a total of over two million. Although many had left the city, including the British ambassador and most other diplomats, many others had entered Paris, and, of course, the military garrison had swelled the numbers. Since no adequate rationing system existed, prices soon began to rise and queues collected outside foodshops. (The modern word queue originated in this siege.) Alcohol remained plentiful and relatively cheap throughout the siege, and, in their idleness, the National Guard consumed vast quantities of liquor.

Considerable amusement was generated by schemes for arming the women of Paris. The most fantastic plan was to equip them with "little india-rubber thimbles, which the women would place on their fingers, each thimble being topped with a small pointed tube containing some Prussic acid. If an amorous Prussian should venture too close to a fair Parisienne, the latter would merely have to hold out her hand and prick him. In another instant he would fall dead!"

Militarily, the first two months of the siege were uneventful. The Germans spent their time digging in and making themselves as comfortable as circumstances permitted. Moltke was obviously determined to play a waiting game and had no intention of launching a major offensive, which might have been bloodily defeated by the great guns of Paris. In this period the French made some minor sorties, the one on September 20 being an offensive reconnaissance to the south of the city. 20,000 men attacked the Prussians, but, although protected by the guns of the great forts of Bicetre and Ivry, the French were repulsed with heavy losses. Trochu's next small sortie was more useful, in that his men drove some Bavarian troops from their outposts in the Chatillon area, and the French returned unmolested to their own lines with 200 prisoners. A large crowd of Parisians assembled on a height overlooking the battlefield to watch this engagement.

Encouraged by this minor triumph, another of these limited sorties was ordered. It took place on October 21 on the western side of Paris between St. Cloud and Mont Valerien; this was one of the most strongly defended sectors, the Prussian headquarters being at Versailles only some 5 miles away. Under the brave personal leadership of General Ducrot, the French fought well for five hours and then retired, having lost about 620 men. What was meant to be little more than an inconclusive skirmish was soon wildly exaggerated until rumor had classed it as a major attempt to break out from Paris. A sardonic eyewitness account shows the kind of emotions that were aroused. He wrote of a "crowd of amateurs who have smuggled themselves outside the walls in ambulance carriages and by all manner of devices, to enjoy the fluctuating emotions of the fight. How keen their sight is to detect the smoke of imaginary French cannons behind the crests in the rear of the Prussian front, pounding the unconscious foe with shells that, with a little ob-

servation and unprejudiced use of the glass, you can see bursting in the ranks of the red trousers (Prussians)." Another strange incident was reported about a British sniper known as the Black Bird. "I saw writhing in agony, and for all the world like a circus clown walking on his knees, an individual very carefully dressed in a black velvet coat and knickerbockers, who had been hit full in the chest by a bullet. . . . He was an Englishman, an eccentric fanatic who made war on his own account as an amateur and as an ally of the Prussians. He was dispatched."

W. H. Russell, *The Times* correspondent famous for his Crimean War dispatches, watched the same engagement from the Prussian side. "The Hotel du Pavillion Henry IV was crowded with Prussians. Everybody in immense excitement. Yet how odd it was, waiters were serving people in the gilded saloon, and groups of officers at their breakfast, discussing what they saw through their field glasses as they ate their meals. The French population were swarming in the few places where they were allowed to congregate, whence they could get a glimpse of the battle. . . . The cries of the people, their exclamations of joy . . . as the action seemed to go in favor of the French, and their low murmurs of grave disappointment as the onward progress of their friends was stayed, and, at last, a retrograde movement was commenced, was something new to me, for never before had I seen a multitude of civilians present as spectators of an actual combat."

In the excitement of the moment, some French civilians became overconfident. In one village, they brought out their hidden shotguns and fired at the Prussian soldiers. The reprisals were ruthless. Nineteen men were arrested, two of whom were executed; all their houses were destroyed, and their village was heavily fined. The Prussians made it mercilessly clear that they would stand no nonsense from the civilian population.

Yet less than a week later, another of these pointless sorties occurred. This time it was an unofficial one. Chaffing at the interminable inaction, a fire-eating general sent out a small group of irregular troops, who surprised the Prussians and captured the lightly held village of Le Bourget, which lies to the north of Paris. Having reinforced them, the general went to Trochu to demand that this triumph be followed up. Although Paris was by now rejoicing at what had been ludicrously exaggerated into a magnificent victory, Trochu himself was angry and embarrassed, since Le Bourget was too isolated to be of military value. With his rigid, soldier-like outlook, Trochu could not appreciate the psychological stimulus that this victory had aroused in the Parisian mind, and he refused to send more troops to defend Le Bourget. A couple of days later, the Prussians subjected the village to a very heavy barrage and then sent in a strong force which drove the French out; 1,200 men were lost in this fruitless affair.

As if this defeat was not enough, Paris officially heard on October 31 that the last French stronghold, the great fortress of Metz, had been starved out: 180,000 French troops had surrendered there, but perhaps more ominously for the Parisians its fall released two German armies, which were directed to join the Siege of Paris.

The cumulative effect of these setbacks was to plunge Paris into the depths of depression. Stories of treason and the "incapacity of our chiefs" began to circulate freely. On October 31, an uprising began. At one stage, this looked as if it would develop into a full-scale revolution when most of the government, including General Trochu himself, was imprisoned in the town hall by a mob in which the more revolutionary National Guard soldiers predominated. This "Red revolt" was so spontaneous that it surprised the extremist leaders themselves, who did not therefore manage to arrive on the scene until it had already got underway. It is one thing, however, to decide to overthrow political leaders, but quite another to form a new and more effective government on the spur of the moment. The resultant chaos of this queer uprising has been graphically described by eyewitnesses. "The square was a forest of rifle butts raised in the air, the metal plates gleaming in the rain. . . . On every face could be seen distress at Bazaine's capitulation at [Metz], a sort of fury over yesterday's reverse at Le Bourget, and at the same time an angry and rashly heroic determination not to make peace. . . . Shouts of the 'Commune forever!' went up all over the square, and fresh battalions went rushing off down the Rue de Rivoli, followed by a screaming, gesticulating riffraff."

A French captain, d'Herisson, was in the midst of the bedlam that night. He described how more and more men of the National Guard crammed into the council chamber, where "their leaders . . . had transformed the baize-covered table into a circus ring, and strode along it treading on the paper and jotting books, upsetting the inkstands and sandboxes; and, as their audience also shouted, nobody could hear them. Trochu, with his two officers still behind his chair, smoked his cigar and watched the coming and going of these spurred or worn heels on a level with his chest."

Indeed, throughout these farcical but dangerous hours when he was a prisoner at the mercy of the hostile mob, Trochu displayed a miraculous calmness. Before disappearing into the town hall to see what he could do on the morning of October 31, Trochu had insisted that no armed help should be sent to free him, unless summoned on written orders from himself. When it became evident, however, that Trochu was being forcibly detained, the fiery General Ducrot began to organize a relief force to march on the town hall. His policy of forcibly crushing this Red revolt commanded widespread support from the loyal middle-class battalions of the National Guard, who had been called out in this emergency. Many Parisians feared that this uprising might lead to another era of terror in Paris, like that of the Commune from 1792 to 1794. Nevertheless, after several hours of great confusion, the proposed loyalist march on the town hall was called off late that night, since, in the nick of time, a compromise had been arranged between the government and the revolutionary leaders. The revolt then fizzled out without a single casualty. As someone caustically said, "It was Trochu's only successful military operation during the whole siege."

Trochu had good reasons for moderation during this uprising. At all cost he had to avoid plunging the seething population of Paris into civil strife, because the Prussians would almost certainly have exploited such an opportunity and attacked the city. As it was, the favorable chances of negotiating a settlement were shattered by this abortive revolution. On October 31, an elderly French statesman, Thiers, had arranged with Bismarck for an armistice, when Paris' food supply was to be replenished; also it appeared that less harsh terms might have been reached over the future of Alsace and Lorraine. But the news of this revolt in Paris encouraged the Prussian commander, von Moltke, and he was adamant that the siege should continue. Bismarck abandoned

the talks on the excuse that the government that Thiers claimed to represent "no longer existed." When it was announced that these negotiations had collapsed, a contemporary stated, "I never remember to have witnessed a day of such general gloom since the commencement of the siege. The feeling of despair is, I hear, still stronger in the army!" Moreover the events of October 31 deepened the gulf between the two main factions in Paris. The majority of the middle class wanted to end the siege as soon as possible and on almost any terms, since they were already more frightened of the Red extremists in their midst than of the Prussians outside the walls. On the other hand, the working-class masses were fanatically determined to resist at all costs and were becoming increasingly suspicious of the loyalty of their middle-class leaders.

By early November Paris had been under siege for about eight weeks. Since this date also marks the middle of the Parisians' ordeal, it is a convenient moment to pause and examine some of the less military aspects of life in the city. Preoccupation with one unlikely object did much to cheer up the besieged: this was the balloon. These unwieldy, unpredictable, flimsy, colorful contraptions played an important part in the keeping up of the morale of Paris.

Montgolfier, a Frenchman, had invented the balloon in 1783. Since then very few technical improvements had been made, and ballooning continued to be a perilous and unpredictable pastime, whose hazards were never indulged in by more than a very small and intrepid band of enthusiasts. Balloons had appeared on the battlefield as early as 1793, when the French had used them to carry dispatches across the enemy lines; static balloons had also been put into the air during the American Civil War. Recently in Metz, unmanned balloons had been employed to send out letters. Nevertheless, it was during this siege that balloons first captured the imagination of the general public by providing, apart from the uncertain pigeon post, the sole, if fragile, link between the Parisians and the outside world.

When Paris was surrounded there were only 7 balloons there, and most of these were so tattered as to be unusable. Before the city capitulated, 65 balloon flights had been made, 30 of these by sailors who had been specially trained for this task in swaying baskets hung from the girders of a railroad station. It was thought they would be less susceptible to airsickness than landlubbers. Incredible though it may seem, 33 of these flights took place before the first fatal casualty occurred, and out of the 65 flights only 5 of the crews were captured by the Prussians. Some remarkably long flights were inadvertently made: 6 balloons came down in Belgium, 4 in Holland, 2 in Germany, and 1 ended up in Norway. Two balloons were blown out to sea and disappeared; the first fatal casualty was from this cause, and a lighthouse keeper at the Lizard just caught a glimpse of the unlucky pilot in this balloon as it headed out into the Atlantic. In all 164 human passengers made the trip from Paris, as did 5 messenger dogs, all of whom failed to return; 380 homing pigeons were carried out, but less than 60 flew back to the city; in addition 11 tons of official dispatches were transported out of Paris. The balloon traffic was very much a one-way affair; no flights from unoccupied France managed to reach Paris, though several gallant attempts were made.

Nearly all the balloons that floated out of Paris had been built there, and two railroad stations

15   *The balloon in which Gambetta escaped from Paris on October 7, 1870. From a photograph by Nadar*

were converted into balloon assembly factories. "At the Gare du Nord the completed balloons were varnished; stretched out, partially inflated, like rows of massive whales . . . each balloon had to have a capacity of 2,000 cubic meters at least, and be capable of lifting 4 people plus an additional 500 kilograms in weight. For each satisfactory product, the factory received 4,000 francs (of which 300 was earmarked for the pilot)."

The perils have been vividly described. "The balloons themselves were constructed simply of varnished cotton, because silk was unobtainable, and filled with highly explosive coal gas; thus they were exceptionally vulnerable to Prussian sharpshooters. . . . In inexperienced hands they had an unpleasant habit of shooting suddenly up to 6,000 feet, then falling back again almost to ground level. Huddled on their baskets . . . devoid of any protection from the elements, the balloonists suffered agonizingly from the cold. . . . Often the aeronauts carried no compass, and, after a few minutes of twisting giddy progress, they had in any case lost all sense of direction."

The balloons were launched either from the summit of Montmartre or from near one of the stations where they were assembled. With no means of steering, everything depended on the wind direction, once the balloon had risen from the ground. By day it was possible to pick out some landmark, but by mid-November all the flights started at night, because Prussian cavalry groups followed the balloons, waiting to seize the occupants when they reached terra firma.

Two balloon flights vitally affected the course of the Siege of Paris. The first occurred on October 7 at 11 A.M., in front of a huge crowd assembled on Montmartre near the present position of the Sacre Coeur Church. The multitude had come to watch their Minister for the Interior leave the city to whip up enthusiasm and support for their cause in parts of France not occupied by the Prussians. The 32-year-old Gambetta was a flamboyant, dissolute, and dominating figure, with his thickly bearded face, hooked nose, long unkempt locks, and "an eye that protruded so terribly from its socket as to lead one to fear lest it should escape altogether. . . ." On this occasion,

Gambetta was visibly very nervous, and even the cheering of the crowd was insufficient at first to reconcile him to the adventures that he was vividly aware must attend his journey. More furry than usual—he was clad in a large fur cloak—Gambetta finally recovered his poise and delighted the crowd by releasing a large tricolor flag as the balloon lifted off the ground.

Gambetta's journey was a most adventurous one. Twice the pilot brought the balloon down, only to discover that they were still in Prussian-occupied territory, but both times they just managed to get airborne before the enemy arrived. The urgency of escaping was increased by the Prussians' threat to execute anyone they caught from a balloon. Eventually, after a four and one-half hour flight, the two men reached a safe enough area to elude the pursuing Prussians. Gambetta made for Tours, in unoccupied France, where he set up an independent government, with himself in supreme power.

The second vitally important flight began silently at midnight on November 24. This balloon was supposed to fly out in a northwesterly direction and land in an unoccupied part of France, near Amiens. The two men on board were entrusted with the secret plans for Trochu's breakout from Paris, scheduled for November 29. The optimistic idea was for them to contact Gambetta in Tours to enable him to coordinate his plans with those of Trochu in Paris. The wind was, however, far stronger than anticipated. After 15 hours the half-frozen aeronauts suddenly saw snow-covered land just below them and they jumped out immediately; their lightened balloon shot up into the clouds and disappeared. After two days they staggered into civilization to discover, to their consternation, that they were in the depths of Norway, 900 miles away from Paris! By a freak of fate, the balloon, complete with its pigeons, was recovered intact, and some fishermen found the basket full of secret documents, which the aeronauts had jettisoned earlier; these were hurriedly sent on to Gambetta, but arrived far too late to influence his plans.

To return to the military events: during the second half of November, Paris buzzed with rumors of a great sortie that was to be made. After the fiasco of the Le Bourget attack, everyone was heartened by the belief that Trochu had a plan. Unfortunately for the Parisians, the whole affair was really much more complicated. True, Trochu did have a plan, but the first one had to be hurriedly altered, while the second one was easily anticipated by the Prussians. In any case the French could never keep a military secret.

It was assumed that a heroic stand by Paris might revive the national spirit, buy time in which new armies in the provinces could be raised to fight the Prussians, and also persuade other countries to help France in her distress. Trochu's original plan had all these objectives in mind. Thus he decided to employ 40,000 picked troops to break out to the west of Paris, where the Prussians were weakest. Once this force had crossed the Seine, it was to march along the north bank of the river, through unoccupied country, to Rouen. There it would securely establish itself in unoccupied territory in Normandy and Brittany, where it could be supplied from overseas and join up with Gambetta's armies on the Loire. The date for this breakout was the third week in November, and the preparations were well advanced when, on November 14, astonishing news reached the city. A French army had defeated the Prussians. Orleans had been retaken by one of Gambetta's newly organized armies; the Parisians were beside themselves with joy, and strangers kissed each other in the street. Only Trochu was dismayed. He quickly realized that he would be compelled to shift the direction of his sortie. On November 18, one of the few pigeons to make a journey safely arrived with a plea from Gambetta that Trochu should strike in a southerly direction toward Orleans to link up with his victorious army. The next day Trochu informed Ducrot, the general in charge of the operation, that the sortie must be transferred to the other side of Paris. Furious though he was, Ducrot rapidly switched his force of 400 guns, 54 pontoons, and 80,000 men, with all their equipment, right across Paris.

Plans for this major breakout had to be hurriedly drawn up. From the outset the French were badly placed, since, to link up with Gambetta's forces at Orleans, the great sortie could be made only from the southeast section of the front. Well aware of this grave French limitation, the Prussians had already constructed some of their strongest defenses in this region and had positioned between Paris and Orleans the armies released by the fall of Metz. After careful thought, Trochu decided that the only, if somewhat remote, chance of success lay in mounting an enormous attack near where the Marne joins the Seine. The final plan was for the main French forces, totaling 100,000 soldiers, to cross the lower Marne at two places by pontoon bridges, which would have to be towed up there from the Seine. At the same time, diversionary attacks with 70,000 men were to be organized on both flanks of the breakout sector, as well as in other parts of the front. These were supposed to lock up the Prussian reserve and prevent any of their troops being switched to oppose the main French forces. In addition, the

great guns in the nearby Paris forts were to protect the attacking troops. The overall plan was a complicated one depending for its success on very careful timing.

General Ducrot had issued a hysterical Order of the Day proclaiming, "I have made up my mind, and I swear before you and before the entire nation: I shall only re-enter Paris dead or victorious. You may see me fall but you will not see me yield ground." The same "do or die" spirit prevailed in other ways. Although it was the end of November, the troops were not given blankets, since these would render them less mobile; instead they carried a six-day supply of food, while the baggage carts were loaded only with ammunition. Certainly morale was high and the National Guard battalions, each with its different gaudy uniform, made a colorful display at a pre-battle review, which included women dressed in "bloomer costumes, plumed hats, tricolor-painted brandy-kegs slung from their hips, and Roman daggers or even little, ivory-handled pistols tucked into their belts!"

An atmosphere of overwrought optimism prevailed, but the sortie was doomed almost from the beginning. Any hope of surprise had disappeared because, over a week earlier, the Prussians had been alerted by the noise of troops and equipment being transferred across the city; furthermore the heavy guns of Paris forts began a prolonged bombardment three days before the sortie was supposed to start; also, the Prussians were fully acquainted with rumors that were circulating inside Paris. Finally the sortie itself had to be postponed for a day, since the level of the Marne rose rapidly, making it impossible to tow the main pontoon bridges into position by November 29, the planned date. Thus most of the assembled troops had to remain in full view of the Prussians for twenty-four hours, while the engineers struggled to get the pontoons in place.

The main assault eventually began at dawn on November 30. At first, things went according to plan. Having crossed the Marne, the French seized two lightly held outposts and it was not until they climbed the slopes beyond that they struck the main defense lines. Though met by a murderous fire from concealed riflemen and supporting guns, the French soldiers attacked bravely, but could make no impression on these positions. By evening they were exhausted and, on December 1, a 24-hour truce was arranged so that thousands of wounded could be brought in. The following day, the Prussians staged a massive counterattack, driving the French back to the riverbank, but there the great guns of the Paris forts temporarily halted the Prussians. Nevertheless, all prospects of success had vanished, and the great sortie had to be miserably abandoned. Shrouded by the early morning mist, Ducrot safely withdrew his troops across the Marne on December 3. In three days the French had lost 12,000 men and gained nothing.

During the confused and tragic events of the great sortie General Ducrot had hurled himself, regardless of his safety, into the most dangerous places to rally and encourage his men. A member of his staff declared: "He is absolutely mad. All day he has been riding a snow-white horse, and he keeps galloping in front of the Prussians." In spite of his suicidal recklessness, Ducrot survived to be taunted about the words of his famous proclamation, and he offered to serve in the ranks, but this was refused.

A curious figure on the battlefield was a defrocked priest "prancing about on horseback in long purple boots and breeches, with a broad-brimmed ecclesiastical hat on his head, a large gold crucifix and a diamond-studded order around his neck, and a huge episcopal ring on his finger. At his side rode a mounted 'bodyguard'. . . . A standard-bearer with a large Red Cross, and several hundred lay Freres Chretiens acted as stretcher-bearers. . . . Contemptuous of the Prussian bullets he rode about the field directing the succor of the wounded."

This sortie brought home to the Parisians, for the first time, the horrors of the battlefield. In stunned silence they watched the thousands of wounded being brought to the hospitals; some were carried in by the Seine boats, some on carriages, and some in ambulances. For the badly wounded the chances of recovery were poor. The main hospital, with 500 patients, was in the Grand Hotel. There a visitor found the wounded "packed three, four, and five in each of the little rooms. . . . Ventilation cannot be said to be imperfect, for there is none, and the dead, as many as fifty at a time, are placed, 'packed like biscuits,' in the center of the gallery into which the rooms open. The stench is something terrible." Antiseptics were nonexistent, and septicemia killed off almost all the amputation cases; even a cut finger in this germ-filled air was supposed to kill a man before he could reach the door!

Many fashionable people had turned their large

houses into self-styled hospitals. They flew big Red Cross flags from their dwellings, and one Englishman counted 15 of these from his bedroom window! From the beginning, the shortage of patients caused great competition for inmates, and the authorities easily lost track of lightly-wounded patients, who frequently never reappeared for duty. For the badly wounded recovery was likely in only one hospital, that run by the American Ambulance team, whose doctors had been trained in the new methods during the recent Civil War. The 200 wounded here were kept in two drafty tents heated only by stoves set in the ground. To the consternation of visiting Frenchmen, cold fresh air circulated vigorously, but four out of five amputation cases lived, whereas in the Grand Hotel four out of five died. Knowledgeable French officers were supposed to go into battle with a card around their necks asking to be sent to the American Ambulance if they were wounded.

From the almost continuous succession of French defeats, it might be imagined that Prussian morale would have been high. But, surprisingly, this was not so, and, after the siege had lasted eleven weeks, they were nearly as despondent as the French. At the start of their victorious campaign, the Prussian generals had overconfidently predicted that their troops would be safely enjoying Christmas 1870 at home. Yet by the first week in December, Paris appeared to be no nearer capitulating, and to many Prussians it seemed as if they were doomed to be bogged down in a long and wearisome siege. Their gloom was increased as new French armies were raised in the unoccupied parts of the country, and even the recapture of Orleans was insufficient to revive Prussian spirits as the winter set in.

The Prussian camp was bedeviled by many quarrels. The most prolonged dispute was largely between the military and the civilians over the best method of conducting the siege. Moltke had originally based his plans on closely investing Paris, which, he considered, would soon be starved into surrender. By early November this policy was clearly not working according to schedule. This caused the civilians, led by Bismarck, to press even more vociferously for Paris to be bombarded. By the middle of December the Prussian generals, too, had become convinced that a bombardment was necessary; only the Crown Prince still opposed it on humanitarian grounds. Since communications were poor, and Moltke insisted on first assembling 250 heavy guns and over 100,000 rounds of ammunition, the bombardment could not in any case begin until early in 1871. This delay did not improve tempers.

Christmas found the German Court and High Command still at Versailles. The little town was crowded with the innumerable kings, princes, dukes, counts, margraves, and landgraves with whom Germany was then so plentifully provided. Inevitably, intrigues abounded, many of which centered around Bismarck, who was actively scheming to unify Germany with the King of Prussia as Emperor. Bismarck also interfered in military affairs, becoming distrusted and hated by the army. The army, too, mistrusted the Crown Prince, whose English wife (Queen Victoria's daughter) was thought to make him too liberal. Moltke was at loggerheads with Roon, the Minister of War, over the shortages of men and materials, which grew more acute as the siege dragged on. Oddly, the activities of the Paris garrison also frightened many Germans, including the

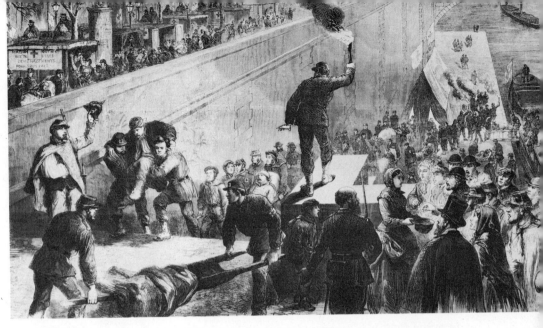

17 *Wounded from the ramparts being landed at the Quay de la Megisserie, Paris (sketch from* The Balloon Post*)*

Prussian king. It was even suggested that the blockade be lifted when the French achieved some successes around Amiens. Furthermore their continued resistance was creating anti-Prussian feeling in the outside world, and this trend disturbed some leaders.

Two other factors contributed to the Prussian sense of depression. The first was the unavoidable sight and smell of the wounded. The ground floor of the huge Palace of Versailles had been turned into a hospital. With the poor medical conditions, gangrene became prevalent, and its ghastly stench hung everywhere around the royal quarters in the upper floors of the palace. Toward the end of the year the number of deaths, from one cause or another, increased sharply, and the elaborately somber military funerals aroused painful emotions in the unwilling spectators who thronged the court. Secondly, this winter was a particularly cold one. Even in December, though comfortably quartered, *The Times* correspondent grumbled that he was "shriveled up with cold." Nevertheless, the Prussian troops were pretty comfortable and well fed. Characteristically, Bismarck complained that the boredom and frustration of his routine led him to excesses of eating and drinking.

Naturally everyone in Paris was very preoccupied by the question of food. By the end of 1870 many people were beginning to go hungry, though the rich were still able to dine well at expensive restaurants. From mid-November, the only meat regularly available was horseflesh, which became more and more expensive, though it has been estimated that 65,000 horses were slaughtered during the siege. Domestic pets were now liable to find their way to the butchers. One Englishman wrote, "I have a guilty feeling when I eat dog, the friend of man. . . . I had a slice of spaniel the other day; it was by no means bad, something like lamb, but I felt like a cannibal. Epicures in dogflesh tell me that poodle is by far the best, and recommend me to avoid bulldog, which is coarse and tasteless." Cats were claimed to be more palatable and were eaten in great numbers. One man was reputed to be "fattening up a huge cat, which he meant to serve up on Christmas Day, surrounded with mice, like sausages." Rat hunting was enjoyed by the National Guard, but being regarded as poisonous, few were eaten. As the animals in the zoo were killed off, exotic dishes like zebra, buffalo, wapiti, camel, and finally elephant, appeared on some menus; almost every restaurant offered elephant steak or black pudding as a New Year's dish. But it was the poor, especially the women and children, who suffered badly, for many shopkeepers and butchers profiteered, charging prices far beyond the means of most working people. The prices of eggs and cheese had gone up 15 times by 1871, and potatoes 6 times. Even bread was scarce and expensive, and a synthetic brand was produced. It was terrible stuff, tasting of "sawdust, mud, and potato skins." All kinds of falsified foods came on to the market, and no one could be sure what they were eating; one butcher was discovered to be selling wolf as lamb. Only wines and liquors could still be bought fairly cheaply, and drunkenness increased very markedly as the siege wore on, especially in the National Guard regiments.

Drink was not only a means of combating hunger but also the cold. By November, coal and coke were unobtainable, and the trees in the parks and along many of the boulevards were ordered to be cut down. This firewood was supposed to be collected into depots for free distribution, but late in December several of these stores were broken open and the wood taken. Other groups of half-frozen Parisians uprooted trees, wooden hoardings, and fences, and even cut down

18 *The carcasses of dogs being sold as meat for human consumption*

telegraph poles; soon nothing that would burn was safe. Yet there was no widespread desire to surrender. One Englishman in Paris marveled, "the people submit to their hard fare, to cold and hunger, and long nights void of amusement, with a cheerfulness that is sublime."

Amazingly, too, a fighting spirit still existed in

Paris. On December 21, Trochu mounted another futile attack on Le Bourget. It was hoped to break out northwards towards Amiens, where some local victories had been gained. Once again the Prussians were waiting, forewarned by the preparations reported in the Paris press and by the prior activity around the Le Bourget sector itself. Subjected to heavy and accurate gunfire, the French columns quickly came to a halt. The night was intensely cold, the unfed troops had no fuel for fires, and 900 cases of frostbite occurred. The following day the almost mutinous soldiers fell back again, having had 2,000 casualties, excluding the frostbite victims.

By Christmas the Prussians had been besieging Paris for fourteen weeks. Nevertheless, although the city was to hold out for another five weeks, hope of relief or victory was dwindling. On December 27, the Prussians began to shell Paris. At first they concentrated on the heavy forts and severely damaged several of these, forcing the garrisons to pull out. On January 5, the bombardment of the city itself began. It was a haphazard affair, since most of the guns were firing at near maximum range, about 7,500 yards. The Parisians were convinced that the Prussians were deliberately aiming at the more easily discernible targets, because churches and hospitals were regularly shelled. Militarily, this three-week bombardment proved to be of little value. The 12,000 shells shot into Paris killed 97, wounded 278, and damaged 1,400 buildings; while French counter-battery fire caused the Prussian gunners several hundred casualties.

The civilian population quickly grew accustomed to the bombardment. Goncourt noted in his journal, "Everybody seems to be leading his usual life." Another eyewitness told how "one is invited for a sou to look through a telescope at the enemy firing off their guns." Some youngsters earned cash selling shell fragments as souvenirs; others found a new game ". . . when they see a man or a woman particularly well dressed, they cry out 'flat, flat! a shell. . . . Down on your faces . . . ' The man, gorgeous in fur, falls flat on the ground—perhaps in the gutter—and the Parisian urchin rejoices." As in all indiscriminate bombardments, strong feelings of anger, and indignation, were aroused by the wanton destruction and loss of life; when a shell landed one night on an orphanage, killing four young boys, a huge crowd attended their funeral.

Although relatively unmoved by its nightly quota of 300 to 400 Prussian shells, Paris could not much longer resist a far deadlier foe, famine. By mid-January, most of the inhabitants were reported to be living on coffee, wine, and bread, though these were becoming more and more difficult to obtain. Also it was still bitterly cold: 1871 was one of the severest winters in history, when even the Seine froze. To add to the misery, new clothes became almost unobtainable, and a foolish proposal to make shirts from old newspapers did little to help. A further irritant was dirtiness, since there was neither soap nor means of warming the water for washing: one man claimed to have worn the same shirt for 39 days. The death-rate from sickness rose steeply. In the first week of the siege it amounted to about 1,250, by the tenth week it was nearly 2,000, and by the eighteenth week (mid-January) it reached almost 4,500, including 1,100 cases of pneumonia and bronchitis. The lack of milk; the filthy, unfiltered drinking water drawn right from the Seine; and the persistent cold sent the infant mortality rate soaring.

Despite all these hardships, extremist elements were agitating for yet another sortie. They pointed out that only about 100,000 out of the 400,000 National Guard had been in action. The feeble government was falling apart, but argued cynically that "the mob would not keep quiet until a certain amount of slaughter was allowed, and that, in order to cure Paris of her fever and reduce her excitement, some pints of blood must be taken from her." Trochu also accepted the need for this sortie, remarking despairingly. "It cannot succeed, but Paris must die on her feet." Moreover he felt that thereby the honor of the army would be safeguarded.

The place chosen was on the western side of the city in the Buzenval—St. Cloud region—where the Prussians were very strongly entrenched. The plan was for about 90,000 men in three columns to make a dawn attack on January 19. The whole situation was even more unfortunate than previous sorties. Fog, a sudden thaw, combined with blocked approach roads, prevented many of the troops from arriving at their starting points on time. Thus the attack was not properly coordinated. The earlier pattern repeated itself in that after some initial progress, the Prussians soon had the situation well under control. Though a few of the attacking units displayed great bravery, others wilted quickly; General Ducrot continued to bear a charmed life, leading the troops forward on his white horse, oblivious to shot and shell. The French had lost 4,000 when Trochu ordered a withdrawal that night; the troops struggled back through guns, limbers, supply wagons, and ambulances, which blocked the muddy narrow lanes. Fortunately, fog shrouded the area till nearly noon, so they were relatively unmolested by the Prussian guns.

On January 22, Trochu was dismissed. On that day an abortive coup d'état was crushed, but not before troops had opened fire. Frenchmen were now killing Frenchmen. The widespread fear of famine added to the growing danger of civil war. The end was approaching rapidly, but even so the militant working class had no intention of surrendering.

On January 23, Favre secretly began negotiations for an armistice with Bismarck. After several days of one-sided negotiations, the armistice terms were signed. To soothe their pride, the French were allowed to fire the last shot. On January 28 Paris surrendered. France lost Alsace and half Lorraine. Most of the army had to hand over its arms, though the Paris National Guard were permitted to retain theirs, a concession which led to much bloodshed in 1871. In addition, the Prussians extorted a huge indemnity and, on March 1, marched ceremoniously into Paris, but their forces only remained in the city for two days.

Paris had held out unaided for 130 days. By modern standards French losses had been light—28,450 casualties, of whom under 4,000 had been killed. But the real killing began in mid-March and lasted for over two months. This was the period of the Paris Commune, when the extremists, many of whom had retained their National Guard arms, seized power from the bourgeois leaders, whom, they felt, had betrayed the cause for which Paris had fought. In putting down this bloody insurrection, 20,000 men, women, and children were slaughtered in one week. Thus what had begun as a siege, in which a brave city defied an invading army, eventually degenerated into a tragic and gruesome civil war.

The Second Great Siege of MALTA
June 1940–November 1942

THE SECOND Siege of Malta was far more prolonged than the first one. It began in June 1940, when the Italians entered the war, and lasted until November 1942, when German–Italian armies started their long retreat from El Alamein to Tunisia.

Between 1565 and 1940 Malta had a relatively peaceful history. The Knights of St. John continued to be an active force in the Mediterranean for about a century after the Great Siege, but as the Turkish menace gradually receded, the Knights became more and more of an anachronism, and the order began to decline rapidly during the second half of the eighteenth century. In June 1798, Napoleon, with a French fleet, occupied the island without any resistance, thus Malta's vast and renowned fortifications, built with such expense and effort, were never tested in action. Napoleon exiled the Grand Master, dispersed the Knights, and looted most of their accumulated treasures; the once world famous Order of St. John gently faded out as a military body. The French proved so unpopular that, later in 1798, the Maltese rose up against them. With British help, the garrison was starved out and surrendered in September 1800. The British took over Malta and turned it into a major naval base during the second half of the nineteenth century. In the First World War, Malta was never attacked and proved a most valuable base during the Dardanelles campaign, when its great harbors and its hospitals were fully used. In 1964 Britain granted Malta independence.

By 1940 about 300,000 lived on Malta, which had become one of the most densely populated areas in the world. The majority of Maltese dwell in Valetta, or in the smaller towns that encompass the capital in a great semicircle. This district is composed of miles of narrow, closely packed streets. The high density of population had convinced experts that Malta was indefensible against air attacks, and virtually nothing was done until just before the outbreak of the Second World War to prepare the island for siege conditions. Even then, very few anti-aircraft guns had been sent to Malta, no fighter force had been organized, no submarine shelter pens had been built into the rock, nor had the more vital parts of the dockyard been put underground. A long-term plan for trying to hold Malta had, however, been agreed to in 1939, but only three airfields and a small radar station had been constructed by the outbreak of war.

Malta was a test case for the effectiveness of sustained aerial bombing. Before the Italian attacks began, no other area had tried to withstand heavy but indiscriminate raids of this sort. Thus no one could foretell how large numbers of defenseless civilians would react to the strain of aerial bombardment, nor was there any method of judging how long the somewhat mercurial Maltese would withstand continuous raids. Furthermore, little experience had been gained about how essential supply services could operate in these circumstances; this was a particularly serious problem for Malta, which produces very little of its own foodstuffs and none of the raw materials needed for heating and lighting purposes. In retrospect, it is clear that the Maltese were introduced relatively gently into the unknown trials of mid twentieth-century siege warfare. After six months of unskillful Italian bombing, they developed the confidence and experience essential for surviving the much more effective German attacks.

The first raids were on June 11 and lasted 12 hours; 23 civilians and 7 soldiers were killed, scores were injured, and considerable damage was done, especially in Valetta and the dockyard areas. Fortunately the Italians sent over no planes next day, when the Maltese were more seriously agitated than at any other time during their siege; work stopped almost everywhere, and a great trek started as those in the built-up areas sought refuge in country districts. Overcrowding soon occurred, and sanitary arrangements broke down in many parts. Yet the Maltese rapidly recovered their normal, cheerful spirit, and there was no widespread defeatism; rather a feeling of anger, mixed with contempt, grew against the Italians.

Although it was not realized until later, Maltese society was naturally well adapted to cope with siege conditions. Families there are large and always retain close ties with each other. Thus nearly everyone has relations scattered over many parts of the island, and the homeless were welcomed immediately. Large-scale evacuation of the danger area was therefore carried out speedily and spontaneously. Though this mass trek to the country produced its own problems, it reduced casualties.

The buildings in Malta, solidly constructed of stone, did not burn, and thus Malta was spared those devastating fires with which incendiary bombs gutted the cities of western Europe. The stone base of Malta meant that safe air raid shelters could be made fairly easily almost anywhere; the grain stores were immune from bomb damage, being deep underground silos hewn out of solid rock and covered with huge circular stones. Finally, with plentiful supplies of easily quarried stone, repairs could be organized without too much trouble.

The more frivolous may argue that the Maltese have long been impervious to the din of high explosives. As any visitor knows, they revel in the noise of explosives: every week at least one village sets off vast quantities of gunpowder, so that the sound effects of air raids are still reproduced with great frequency. But for nearly two and a half years, the Maltese were provided with free "bangs" on a scale previously undreamt of.

About a week after the first Italian air raid took place, a tiny British fighter force took to the air to defy the attackers. It consisted of 4 ex-naval Gladiator biplanes, which were very soon reduced to 3 machines that earned worldwide fame as *Faith*, *Hope*, and *Charity*; the courageous volunteer pilots who flew them were not even trained as fighter pilots. For several weeks, these 3 aircraft and 40 assorted anti-aircraft guns were all that Malta possessed to defend herself against an Italian airfleet over 200 strong, based a mere 60 miles away in Sicily.

An eyewitness wrote of these pilots, "Day after day with our hearts in our mouths we used to follow those three little planes as they spiraled up into the clear blue sky high above us. Everyone of the pilots was known to us, and we used to follow their maneuvers with breathless interest. When they disappeared out of view in pursuit of some of the retreating bombers—remember . . . they did not have time to get them coming in—the whole island used to stand and wait for their return, counting them in until all 3 had safely landed. For many weeks these Three Musketeers formed the sole aerial defense of Malta."

In these early days of the siege, the worst deprivation for the British was the lack of mail, and this became almost unendurable as the German raids on England grew heavier. One of the garrison wrote, "It wasn't fully appreciated how desperately short England was of airplanes, and it was universally considered that at least one plane might be spared to visit Malta, if only once a week, with news of their families, who were then beginning to face the ordeal of the Battle of Britain." No British newspapers ever arrived in the island, and BBC broadcasts assured the garrison everyday that 400 German bombers had caused no damage to England. Inevitably it proved a terrible strain for the British to be cut off from their homeland when it was so seriously threatened by invasion.

In July, 4 Hurricane fighters arrived, to swell the total of British aircraft to 7, and during the next weeks 2 aircraft were lost in combat. These RAF pilots so impressed the Italian bomber pilots that they soon only operated from a great height with a fighter escort, and the Italians estimated that 25 fighter aircraft were defending Malta.

During the second half of 1940, the Italians continued to attack regularly from the air, but the island soon adjusted itself to these visitations. As Miss Dobbie, the governor's daughter, recollected, "In looking back on these first months in the island, they seem curiously isolated from the sterner times that followed. There was indeed a war on—there were enough mild raids to bring that to one's notice—but the only other constant reminder of it was the petrol rationing." And, as she found, the bicycle was the best means of transport, since all buses were terribly overcrowded.

The Royal Navy soon came to the conclusion that they had the measure of the Italian fleet and air force. Between August and December several convoys were successfully brought in and out of Malta, and supplies and reinforcements were built up. Despite the great shortage of fighter aircraft in Britain (the Battle of Britain was being fought), some more Hurricanes were sent. Normally these were flown off carriers, and it could be a hazardous business, especially for inexperienced pilots. On one occasion only 4 from an original group of 12 Hurricanes arrived; the pilots had set their cruising speed too high and thus ran out of fuel; one of those who did land in Malta had a mere 2 gallons of gas left, perhaps 4 minutes of flying time! Also flown into Malta were 3 Maryland aircraft. The pilots of these long-range reconnaissance planes soon began to bring back invaluable information about the movements and dispositions of the Italian fleet. Using photographs taken by the Marylands, the Navy planned and carried out a devastating aerial torpedo attack on the Italian fleet in Taranto during November. Malta had thus begun to hit back at the enemy.

Malta was soon to suffer heavily for helping the British to gain sea and land victories over the Italians. Early in December 1940, the small British army in Egypt began an offensive, which continued with ever-growing success throughout January and early February 1941. So overwhelming was the defeat of the Italian army that it seemed as if it might be expelled from North Africa altogether; for, if the British had managed to reach Tripoli, they might have then persuaded the French in Tunisia and Algeria to join with them against the Italians to finish them off completely. In these circumstances, Mussolini had no option but to accept German help. Hitler decided to bolster up the demoralized Italian army in North Africa by sending over a small but powerful armored force, under Rommel. This could not, however, begin to reach North Africa before the middle of February.

Nevertheless, if the Axis (German–Italian alliance) was to be saved in North Africa, very swift and effective action had to be taken. Hitler took the necessary first step at once. Early in January 1941, Fliegerkorps X, consisting of about 175 aircraft, was rushed from Norway to Sicily. The experienced German pilots immediately and suddenly transformed the situation in the Mediterranean. Using JU 87 Stuka dive bombers together with long-range bombers, they repeatedly attacked a Malta convoy while it was passing through the Narrows between Sicily and Tunisia. This was a most important convoy, since 3,000 tons of seed potatoes and 4,000 tons of ammunition were among the stores in the 5 merchant ships; the German attention was, however, largely directed at the new aircraft carrier *Illustrious*, which was a part of the escort. In spite of determined attacks, the badly damaged carrier limped into Valetta Harbor. On January 16, 250 German and Italian aircraft began a series of raids on Malta. At first these were aimed at the *Illustrious*, but fortunately bad weather made flying impossible for a few days, and, under cover of darkness, she slipped away, partly repaired. Later heavier and more frequent attacks were concentrated on the dockyard, where some deep shelters had been constructed, on the airfields, and on the island indiscriminately. An antiaircraft gunner stationed on top of the old Fort of St. Angelo described these attacks. "Bombs were dropped in and around all the creeks, causing terrific clouds of dust, flying masonry, and iron. Although I did not see it myself, it was stated that a motorcar complete went sailing over the top of us. The dust often blinded our view but the dive bombers always came on . . . like hawks looking for prey.

"The sight was one never to be forgotten, the bursts of the heavies, the red tracers of the Bofors, and light machine guns, and the illuminations made by the crashing planes all adding to the splendor of the day.

"Although tragic, I must say that it is very exciting and good sport to be having a crack at a dive bomber. You lose all sense of fear and self-preservation while it lasts. You get the same feeling as being at a football final."

The pilots were daily fighting an unequal contest. Sometimes only 8 Hurricane fighters could be found to combat 50 or more enemy bombers escorted by 20 to 30 fighters. Nevertheless, although the fighter pilots were outnumbered and the anti-aircraft gunners were continually bombed and strafed, they always managed to hit back. Thus the Germans never achieved that unchallenged supremacy that would have enabled them to destroy their targets in a leisurely and methodical manner.

Even with things at their blackest, some compensations could be found, and one of these was German punctuality. One eyewitness remarked, "The raids came so regularly as to be almost a matter of routine, and people became less and less afraid of them." Amusing incidents also occurred, as when three servicemen were trapped unhurt in an undamaged bar by a bomb that destroyed a neighboring building. Before they could be released and to keep their morale up, they made full use of the many unbroken bottles. When they were reached they were so drunk that their rescuers had to carry them out on stretchers, through the reverent salutes of a sympathetic crowd.

Malta was constantly expecting to be invaded. With the few ill-equipped forces available, it was hopeless to try to hold the island of Gozo. Not even Malta was thought to be defensible, and the main landward bastion was based on the Victoria lines that run along an escarpment at the northeastern end of the island. These positions had been originally constructed in the nineteenth century, and overlook the low-lying country around St. Paul's Bay, facing towards Sicily. It was found that a high wall on the Victoria lines could be used as a simple, early warning system, acting as a kind of baffle-board to reflect the sound of aircraft engines being run up on the Sicilian airfields. Some listeners became so skillful that they could judge, fairly accurately, the numbers of aircraft being prepared. Equally satisfactory results could be obtained by placing one's ear against the rock in the Hypogeum, the ancient underground rock tomb near Valetta.

In April conditions improved when some of the more modern Hurricanes were flown in. The Navy was less fortunate. It suffered heavily when several of its surface craft were sunk and damaged by the many mines, which were dropped around the entrance to the Grand Harbor. Late in May, the German raids ceased. Unknown to those in Malta the Luftwaffe had been switched to the Balkans to help the German army in its attack on Russia. This withdrawal of the Luftwaffe was the answer to the petition of an old lady who, during a heavy German raid, was heard to pray, "O Holy Mother, send over the Italians." From June to the end of November, there were only a few high-flying Italian night bombers, which did little damage. Life now returned to a fairly normal pattern, and food became more plentiful with the arrival of two big convoys, one in July and the other in September.

The punishment Malta received during 1941 was only one side of the picture. As in the time of the Knights, the island's unique strategic position in the Mediterranean again enabled it to hit back at its enemies. This new counteroffensive started slowly. In December 1940, three small U-class submarines arrived in the Grand Harbor and were soon joined by more. (It was impossible to operate larger submarines in the shallow waters around Malta, Sicily, and Libya.) By March 1941, these submarines were regularly sinking the Axis supply vessels that sailed from Italy to bring men and supplies to Rommel's forces in the Libyan Desert. For instance, late in May the *Upholder*, commanded by Lieutenant Wanklyn, broke through the Italian naval escort to sink the big liner *Conte Rosso*, which was carrying 2,729 soldiers and crew; the *Upholder* was then attacked for two hours while 40 depth charges were dropped on her; for this exploit Wanklyn received the Victoria Cross. Nevertheless, the submarine losses were heavy, and by August, three of the U-class boats had been lost, as well as two of the other larger mine-laying submarines based on Malta; the *Upholder* herself survived until April 1942, when she was sunk on her twenty-fifth patrol!

Even the relatively peaceful summer of 1941 had its alarms. On the night of July 25, the alertness of the defenders was tried out with dramatic suddenness. The first big convoy of the year had just arrived in the Grand Harbor, when the Italians decided to stage a raid against it from the sea. Under the cover of the noise of an air attack, E boats (motor-torpedo boats) and one-man submarines were to creep inside the harbor boom at night to destroy the supply vessels before they were unloaded. The Italian Air Force, however, did not turn up, while the garrison at Fort St. Elmo heard the sound of engines and spotted the E boats. At once the Maltese coastal gunners on top of the fort opened fire, to be joined by all the other guns within range. As an eyewitness recalled, "Bofors (light anti-aircraft guns) were firing out red balls of fire, which were bouncing off the sea and searchlights were sweeping across the harbor mouths. Green streaks of light from the twin 6-pounders of the coastal defenses were intermingling with Bofors tracers and darting up and down in the most

fantastic curves." In under five minutes all of the 17 one-man submarines were sunk as well as five E boats. The only damage was to a span of a bridge in the harbor mouth, which was hit by a torpedo and collapsed, blocking the harbor more fully. At dawn Hurricanes flew out to damage some of the retreating E boats. In spite of its complete failure, the Italians claimed that this raid was partly successful!

Throughout this period Malta was fortunate in having a remarkable commander in the person of the governor, Lieutenant-General Sir William Dobbie, who was an engineer officer in his early sixties. He was admirably suited to this job, being calm, confident, resourceful, brave, and deeply religious. Although he was a Protestant, this difference in religious beliefs between him and the Maltese was successfully bridged by his obvious personal sincerity and by his deep faith in the power of prayer. With his calm presence and his personal bravery, he was a tower of strength in 1940 and 1941.

When the Luftwaffe left for Russia, British bombers could safely return to the Maltese airfields. For the next six months they battered away at the Axis supply vessels. By day, about 20 twin-engined Blenheim bombers and Beaufort torpedo-carrying aircraft ranged around Malta attacking shipping. They suffered heavy losses, since the pilots had to go in very low to hit their targets, which meant they were extremely vulnerable to fire from the well-armed enemy ships. On each mission up to one-third of the planes were shot down by anti-aircraft fire. By night, 30 of the longer-range Wellington bombers, aided by a couple of dozen torpedo or mine-carrying biplanes of the fleet air arm (Swordfish and Albacores) pounded away at the ships by dropping bombs and mines; the harbors at Naples and Tripoli were also attacked regularly. Air attacks were thus kept up almost around the clock.

So unchallengeable had become Malta's supremacy over the Italians, that late in October a naval surface force was sent there. It consisted of two cruisers, *Aurora* and *Penelope*, and two destroyers. Under Captain Agnew's brave command, they successfully intercepted several convoys during the following six weeks.

In November this combination of surface, underwater, and air strikes resulted in 63 percent of all the cargoes shipped to the enemy forces in Libya being sunk en route. By the middle of December 1941, the British Eighth Army had almost driven Rommel's forces out of eastern Libya. Ciano, the Italian Foreign Minister, wrote in his diary, "Our merchant fleet will not last another year at this rate." Admiral Doenitz, the chief of the German navy, is recorded to have said in September, "Malta must be destroyed." Rommel himself was almost in despair at the persistent losses of his much-needed supplies and equipment. During 1941 the Italians lost a total of 191 ships, amounting to 820,000 tons; a high proportion of these sinkings were directly attributable to the naval and air forces based on Malta.

When flying became greatly restricted on the Russian front, the Germans once more quickly transferred many aircraft from there to Sicily. About 600 front-line airplanes were put under the command of Marshal Kesselring, who soon began an all-out offensive against Malta. This time he was determined to reduce the island to impotence by bombing. From January 1942 until the latter part of June, waves of German and Italian planes attacked Malta daily. The intensity of the blitz can be judged from the fact that from January 1 to July 24, 1942, Malta had only one day without a raid, and there were air attacks on 154 consecutive days. The worst month was April, when 6,000 tons of bombs were dropped on the island; this total exceeded the weight of bombs dropped on London during the 1940 blitz. Sometimes up to 300 enemy aircraft appeared over the island. With all this bombing, the destruction of houses in Malta assumed terrible proportions, and living conditions for most of the population became appalling.

During the first five months of 1942 the defenses were almost overwhelmed. The main burden fell on the gunners, who were on duty almost continuously. So busy were they that some of their barrels were literally worn smooth by the constant firing, but with no replacements available, these guns had to continue to shoot as best they could. Inevitably ammunition had to be drastically rationed: by the middle of April each anti-aircraft gun was limited to 15 rounds per day—an amount that a Bofors gun can fire off in 7 seconds! These restrictions were only relaxed when a new batch of fighters was about to land and had to be given special protection. In April alone the anti-aircraft gunners claimed 102 enemy aircraft shot down, but though they did all that was within their power, the gunners could do little more than deter the attackers and put them off their aim. They could not hit the Germans hard enough to stop them continuing to raid the island. A few extracts from a diary kept by an anti-aircraft officer give a picture of day-to-day life.

THURSDAY, FEBRUARY 5, 1942
Small raids continue incessantly night and day.

83

WEDNESDAY, MARCH 4

The arrival of 18 Spitfires and a squadron of Beaufighters for night defense has put new life into the island. Morale has shot up 100 percent, and the civilians now hang about outside the shelters watching for the Spitfires to engage.

THURSDAY, MARCH 26

Very intense air activity with more dive bombing by JU 88s and Stukas on the Grand Harbor. Two large boats were hit. Spitfires and Hurricanes were up, and they engaged the enemy bombers, but these came in such number as to bewilder our fighters.

FRIDAY, MARCH 27

Damage in the Grand Harbor was pretty extensive. Of all the convoy that arrived here now, nothing remains.

TUESDAY, APRIL 7

The heaviest raids yet experienced. Marsa creek heavily bombed, but a submarine concealed among the barges remained unscathed.

SATURDAY, APRIL 25

Beer has been cut down to one bottle per man per week, and there is great difficulty in getting wines.

Malta's most desperate need was for more fighters. The persistent German attacks on the airports had damaged or destroyed so many British aircraft that few were fit to fly, and these losses continued to mount in spite of the special stone "blast pens" in which the aircraft were housed. In the first 4 months of 1942, it was rare for more than 15 fighters to be serviceable in the morning, while by the evening the numbers might be down to as low as 1 or 2; this was hope-less odds against the 100 or so enemy fighters that were always sent over to protect their bombers. The strain on the pilots was almost unbearable, some of them flying up to 5 operational sorties in one day.

Some grim humor could still be extracted from the situation. A fighter pilot recorded in his diary, "Italian radio claimed 13 'spits' destroyed here yesterday; there were 9 airborne all day." A trick had been played on the German fighters and an eyewitness recalled, "There were several fighter pilots with me in the operations room, one of them was a Canadian with an unmistakable voice. I put him at the microphone at a standby radio set and proceeded to give him dummy orders. He replied as if he were flying his fighter. This, we suspected, caused a cry of 'Achtung Spitfeuer' to go over the German radio. In any case two Messerschmitt 109s enthusiastically shot each other down, without any British aircraft being airborne."

During the early part of 1942, the fighter pilots were further handicapped because the Hurricanes were outclassed by the Messerschmitt 109 fighters, with which the Germans protected their bomber groups. If the air defenses were to become effective, Spitfires had to be got on to Malta. The old aircraft carrier HMS *Eagle* was chosen for this task, and set off from Gibraltar early in March. The Spitfires flew off her decks when she was over 200 miles away and landed safely in Malta. For the next few months a shuttle service of carriers, chiefly the *Eagle* and the large American carrier *Wasp*, steamed eastwards out of Gibraltar until they reached a point where the fighters, equipped with extra drop tanks, could reach the island. Even then disaster could intervene. One batch of Spitfires was destroyed before even going into action, as the Germans bombed the airfield as soon as they landed. Nevertheless, by the end of May, sufficient reinforcements of Spitfires had been flown in for the British pilots to have gained the upper hand over the Germans.

Malta had been christened the "fighter pilots' paradise" partly because the pilots were so fully occupied and partly because so few lived to tell the tale: 800 Spitfires were lost at the cost of 518 pilots, but by the end of 1942 over 900 German and 600 Italian aircraft had been destroyed. Pierre Closterman interviewed "Screwball Beurling," one of the few survivors of this long conflict. This young Canadian sergeant left the carrier *Eagle* with a group of 32 Spitfires. Of the approach to Malta, Closterman wrote, "Details became discernible—the seething bay of Marsa Xlokk, the deep gash of Valetta harbor, ringed by tiers of flat-roofed houses, the web of hedges and stone walls cutting up the arid fields. Further on, the leprous sore of the main airfield, riddled with bomb craters. . . .

"Accustomed to the orderly arrangements of English airfields, Beurling was taken aback at the sight of this stretch of ground, 5 miles long, with bits of runway everywhere and sinuous tracks disappearing into underground shelters This extraordinary airfield was really three— Luqa, Safi, and Hal Far—connected by two gravel strips. . . .

"However serious the damage, there was always some serviceable corner left. Enormous heaps of stones were dotted here and there for filling in the new craters as soon as the raid was over. All round the perimeter, except where it ran along the cliff, there was a series of bays with thick walls, to protect parked planes from splinters. Remains of burnt-out wings and fuselages were scattered about everywhere.

"The field was swarming with men . . . Beurling just followed the others down and found himself on a bumpy track at the end of which stood a group of soldiers waving him on. As he came past, two of them grabbed hold of his wing tips, while a third jumped on the wing and caught hold of his shoulder.

"In the end he found himself in a kind of rabbit burrow formed by heaps of petrol cans filled with sand. Before he had time to draw breath he was surrounded by a gesticulating crowd of extraordinary looking individuals, unshaven and dressed in relics of the uniforms of all three services. The fitter who had guided him in switched his engine off. Three muscular types grabbed the tail and swung the plane round so that it faced the airfield again. More men came staggering up with cans of petrol. . . ." Beurling and his kit were unceremoniously bundled out of the plane, which was immediately refueled and rearmed, and another pilot leaped into the cockpit.

This sortie was over in 10 minutes, and the planes came back, "two with damaged undercarts had to bellyland, while a third with a good square yard of wing missing did a ground loop and turned arse over tip."

Beurling now had a chance to look around, and Closterman continues his account. "The Mess was an old chalk quarry, a smoke tunnel, 100 yards long and emerging straight into a coast road . . . there was insufficient current to work the fans; what there was of it was reserved for the dim bulbs and the water pumps. The air was heavy with the smell of sweat, cooking, and tobacco smoke. . . . As there was no coal, the cookers were fed on old sump oil—a damaged aircraft was a godsend, as it meant hot soup for two or three days! . . .

"About 150 NCOs from the fighter and torpedo-bomber squadrons slept and ate there. The officers were not better off. Their billets had been bombed three times, and they lived in a kind of gypsy encampment composed of tarpaulins and corrugated-iron sheets stretched over remains of walls. . . .

"Lunch consisted of 5 shrivelled olives, 1 slice of fried corned beef, 4 ounces of bread, 3 semi-ripe dried figs, and a cup of tea. Pilots also had a right to 2 tablespoonfuls of raw shredded carrots soaked in cod-liver oil, for the essential vitamins, and a sulphur pill against diarrhea."

Beurling was still too shaken by his eventful arrival to have any appetite.

Beurling was soon in the thick of it. That afternoon he prepared in his Spitfire to go up on his first sortie. Closterman takes up the narrative. "The sun beat down on the pilots. It was like being in an oven. The fitters had spread damp canvas over the hoods to give them some sort of protection, before themselves taking shelter in the shade under the wings. . . . Several hundred soldiers and Maltese, sweat pouring off them, were at work trying to repair the damage of the morning's raid. . . .

"What heat! And at 20,000 feet there were going to be 27 degrees of frost, but a stroke would be the result if they put on fur-lined boots or anything in the shape of underclothes now.

"An hour later, his plane refueled and rearmed, Beurling took off again with another flight, to intercept a formation of 30 Junkers and 87 Stukas, escorted by 110 Messerschmitts! The Luftwaffe meant at all costs to sink the *Welsh-man*, which had just arrived with a cargo of aviation spirit and AA ammunition. Every Spitfire and Hurricane on the island that was capable of flying at all went up." By the end of October, Beurling was credited with having destroyed 28 enemy aircraft. Such was the hectic dangerous life of the Malta fighter pilots, many of whom were suffering from a form of dysentery popularly termed "Malta Dog."

In May the British government recalled General Sir William Dobbie. Since he had so fully identified himself with Malta and the Maltese, this change of governors at the height of the struggle was naturally resented by many. The best explanation of the reason for Dobbie's recall is given by Churchill. He wrote, "Disturbing news in April arrived about General Dobbie. Up to this moment he had been magnificent, and from all parts of the Empire eyes were turned on him—a Cromwellian figure at the key point. But the long strain had worn him down. I received this news with my deep regret, and I did not at first accept what I was told."

The main criticism of General Dobbie was his lack of organizing drive. In March, the only two merchant ships which had managed to get through safely to Malta were sunk in the Grand Harbor 48 hours after their arrival, no attempt having been made to unload them during the two previous nights when the air attacks almost ceased. The RAF commander, angry at this inaction, had sent airmen especially to unload most of the RAF cargo, but this was about all that had been removed before the vessels were sunk. Dobbie's successor was Lord Gort, the governor of Gibraltar. So critical was the situation, however, that Gort brought with him surrender terms, just in case the worst should come to the worst.

The sustained heroism of Malta had gripped the imagination of the British people, themselves so recently threatened by invasion and still victims of air attacks. In their mind, this little island had become a visible symbol of undaunted resistance to the Axis powers. Thus the award of the George Cross to Malta in April (before the recall of General Dobbie) was a stroke of genius. This medal, together with the dispatch of Spitfires, an aircraft already endowed with an almost mystical significance, proved that Britain would not abandon Malta without the most intense struggle.

Although the air defenses had gained the mastery of the skies over Malta, a new crisis faced the island in the summer of 1942. Starvation was now a real threat. By June the authorities in Malta knew that the island would have exhausted its bread supplies by October. Somehow a garrison of 30,000, half British and half Maltese, and 275,000 Maltese had to be fed. For this purpose alone, 15,000 tons of supplies were needed every month. This amount could not be provided by individual ships that managed to slip through the enemy blockade, like the *Breconshire*, which had made several trips before being sunk in March; fast minelayers like HMS *Welshman* continued to bring in supplies unescorted, but such little vessels could only carry 340 tons of stores, which had largely to be confined to ammunition. As in the most critical months of 1941, submarines were again employed. They could, however, only carry fuel strapped to their hulls in containers, and some ammunition in their torpedo tubes; they also filled any space with tins of food, so that the cramped quarters in a submarine were even more constricted.

For the sailors the situation got steadily worse as 1942 wore on. In the previous year a remarkable total of 30 out of 31 supply ships had safely reached the island. From January to July 1942, on the other hand, of the 30 supply ships that sailed for Malta, 10 had been sunk on the journey, 10 more had to turn back damaged, while of the remaining 10 that reached Malta, 3 were sunk in the harbor there before being unloaded; thus only 7 out of 30 vessels had succeeded in unloading their supplies for Malta. The naval losses were also very high: 1 cruiser and 8 destroyers were sunk while escorting the convoys; this was 2 more than the total naval losses during the Dunkirk evacuation! In addition, many naval vessels had been damaged on the convoy work to Malta.

In mid-June an attempt was made to run two convoys to Malta. The one from Egypt soon encountered terrible opposition and, with the Eighth Army falling back to El Alamein, the Desert Air Force could give it little protection. All the surviving ships of this eastern convoy were forced to return to Egypt, and nothing came of this effort. Simultaneously the other convoy set out from Gibraltar, but only 2 of the 6 merchant ships got through, carrying 15,000 tons; as they sailed into Malta, protected by fighter aircraft, the walls of the Grand Harbor were lined with cheering crowds. Under Lord Gort's able and energetic direction, these supplies were unloaded in four and a half days without loss. Starvation had been temporarily averted. This had been, however, a most expensive operation; the British losses totaling 1 cruiser, 5 destroyers, 2 minesweepers, 6 merchant ships, and over 20 aircraft; in addition 13 other vessels had been damaged. Admittedly the enemy also suffered losses in ships and planes.

There were other perils developing. In May, photographs showed that the Axis were assembling forces in Sicily for an invasion of Malta, planned for the end of June, after Rommel had captured Tobruk. Given the name Operation Hercules, it was to have been a combined German and Italian invasion, with the Germans providing half the airborne forces, under General Student, who had successfully led the invasion of Crete; the Italians were to have been solely responsible for the seaborne side, as well as supplying all the vessels. In fact the proposed Operation Hercules soon ran into disagreements about the exact roles to be played by the two countries, and the whole plan was never fully worked out. Though Kesselring pressed hard for this invasion, Rommel's cancellation of Operation Hercules in June was received with relief by most Germans and Italians. The reason for the abandonment of this invasion was that, after capturing vast quantities of stores in Tobruk, Rommel decided that he could break through and seize Egypt without needing to finish off Malta first. For those in Malta the disasters to the British forces in the desert made it a very grim summer, and many were pessimistic about their chances of survival.

In July there was again a danger that Malta would be starved into submission. Bread is the staple diet of the Maltese, which they eat by the loaf rather than by the slice. Now it was rationed to less than ¾ pound per day per person and was of poor quality. Flour was unobtainable, as was butter; no tea, nor milk (except for children), nor jam (but some marmalade), nor rice, nor sugar was officially available; one bar of laundry soap had to last two weeks. Now and then potatoes and vegetables could be bought.

19 SS Talbot *loaded with ammunition, burning in Grand Harbor after being hit in an aerial attack in March 1942. There was great danger of an explosion and at great personal risk the fire was put out in time*

For the wealthier people, eggs cost from 1s 6d to 3s 6d each, rabbits about £1 10s, and chickens much more (these prices must be multiplied about three times to bring them to 1967 values). Water was short, the mains and reservoirs being hit so often that in hot weather many had to wait hours to obtain a gallon or two from a water cart. Almost as serious was the lack of fuel. Enough electricity could be generated to supply only the hospitals and a few other essential services. There was no coal, so no gas. For cooking, a family of five obtained about ¾ gallon of paraffin every two weeks. As may be imagined, any wood from bomb-damaged houses was quickly removed. The only bright spot was that 35,000 goats were rounded up, and their milk bottled centrally in hygienic conditions, which ended the undulant fever, but by the autumn most of the goats had to be slaughtered, since there was nothing to feed them on.

The sailors, soldiers, and airmen were little better off than the civilians. They did get three thin slices of corned beef twice daily to give them added strength for their hard manual labor, but they had less bread than the civilians. There were many examples of soldiers losing 28 pounds in weight, since they had to exist on 2,000 calories per day and Churchill remarked on Lord Gort's thinness at the Cairo Conference in August. Of course a black market did exist, but it did not have a great deal to offer except occasional goat's meat and stolen rations. People in Malta considered that it was "safer to have a £5 note about than a packet of biscuits."

As for luxuries, cigarettes were rationed to about 40 per week. With no fuel the breweries could not work, so Malta was beerless. At first there were fairly adequate supplies of liquor,

20 *A grocer sets up shop amid the debris below the walls of the city of Valetta*

but by 1942 most of this had been drunk and only rum and the local wine was obtained fairly easily. For nearly a year no mail arrived, so the 15,000 British troops were cut off from their families, and this siege seemed a "life sentence in prison without hope of reprieve."

With about eight weeks supply of food left, drastic steps had to be taken if Malta were to survive, and it was decided to run one large convoy from Gibraltar. This was to consist of 14 of the finest and fastest merchantmen, 2 of which were American. To escort these valuable cargo ships, a fleet of naval vessels was assembled consisting of 3 aircraft carriers, with 72 machines on them, 24 destroyers, 3 cruisers, 3 anti-aircraft cruisers as well as 2 battleships *Rodney* and

Nelson. It was too risky to send most of the naval vessels beyond the Sicilian Narrows, so for the last part of the voyage the escorting vessels were to be reduced to 3 cruisers, 3 anti-aircraft cruisers, and 12 destroyers; it was, however, anticipated that from then onward the 175 aircraft based in Malta could provide some protection.

The enemy realized the importance of this convoy and concentrated a tremendous force. Over 600 (some authorities reckon nearly 1,000) aircraft were positioned along the convoy route, as well as 21 submarines, 6 cruisers, 12 destroyers, and 23 motor torpedo boats. In addition a new minefield was laid. Only the Italian warships were not to be risked in this encounter. Thus the passing of this convoy through from Gibraltar to Malta became a major air–sea battle. On its success depended not only the fate of Malta but also, to some extent, Rommel's army. This was now far away in Egypt, with very extended lines of communications, and from Malta, submarines and aircraft were again sinking more and more of Rommel's few remaining supply ships. The island had to be knocked out, otherwise, as Kesselring had predicted, the Germans could not finally defeat the Eighth Army and go on to Alexandria and Cairo.

This large convoy left Gibraltar on August 10 and spent over three days on the voyage. It was an epic battle, which can only be briefly told here. Within 24 hours the aircraft carrier *Eagle*, veteran of so many fighter-supply trips to Malta, had been sunk. In the next 2 days, 9 of the 14 merchant ships, including the 2 American vessels, were sunk, as were 2 of the 6 cruisers with others badly damaged. Into Valetta on August 13 steamed 3 merchant ships with scarred and blis-

tered sides. One ship had a great gash, which had been sealed by using some of her cargo of flour. The *Times of Malta* has described the excitement. "The first way most people heard of this great event was when a cry went up, 'the convoy is here', from boys in the harbor area. The news spread like wildfire. At once huge crowds surged towards the Grand Harbor and filled every vantage point." Bands played, and the crowds cheered and wept as the ships came in; many of those present had been anxiously following the progress of the convoy, whose terrible ordeal had been only too graphically broadcast by the Italian radio. For the Maltese, their relief at seeing these ships in their harbor was too poignant for words.

To everyone's surprise, the next day a single merchant ship sailed in; an eyewitness wrote that "this ship had a crashed JU 87 (Stuka) on her deck and a hole in her bows. But this was not all. Slowly approaching Malta, the half-submerged tanker *Ohio* was struggling to keep afloat. She had destroyers lashed to her, and other destroyers circling to protect her, while overhead, Spitfires attacked the enemy bombers that were trying to finish off the *Ohio*." One writer has described how "time and again the wires parted, only to be renewed by the sleep-starved sailors. Other difficulties, too many to be recounted, were dealt with by splendid seamanship. It was, indeed, by little short of a miracle of skill and endurance that the *Ohio* was finally got into the Grand Harbor of Valetta." On the feast day of the Assumption, August 15, she reached safety; 15,000 tons of fuel oil and kerosene was salvaged from her torn hull before she was scuttled. Malta was temporarily saved.

Thirty-two thousand tons of supplies now had

21 *After the Blitz. Old Bakery Street, Valetta*

22 *At Ta Qali airfield, Air Vice-Marshal Sir Hugh Pugh Lloyd, Air Officer Commanding, is seen beside a Spitfire with the Hon. Mabel Strickland (then editor of the* Times of Malta) *and the late Mr. J. Olivieri Munroe (then editor-in-chief of the* Times of Malta)

to be unloaded, and elaborate preparations were made to do this in only 3 days. Though the rations were still very meager, Malta could now last until mid-November. But the cost had become enormous; out of the 3 convoys of 35 merchant ships that set out for Malta between March and August 1942, only 7 ships had been safely unloaded.

Now the submarines and aircraft based on Malta went on to the offensive with ever-mounting success. During the autumn of 1942, their sinking of Axis shipping helped immobilize Rommel's army on the Alamein line, while the continuing presence of British power in Malta locked up scores of German aircraft in Sicily, thus depriving the Germans and Italians in the desert of much-needed support from the air. So seriously did the Germans rate this revival of Malta's strength that, in October, Kesselring made yet another effort to knock out Malta by aerial attack. But with 100 Spitfires available, the RAF very soon shot the raiders out of the sky.

Although the defenders had won a resounding victory, the danger of starvation remained. By October the shortage of food was acute. Miss Mabel Strickland, a leading politician, recalled that by then, all poultry, pigs, and cattle had been slaughtered, for there was nothing to feed them on. A few horses on strict rations, and goats feeding on the countryside, still existed. Fishing was not possible, since there was no bait and almost every fishing boat had been destroyed. By November the daily ration had been reduced to 6 ounces of bread, 1 ounce each of sugar, corned beef (about 1 slice), and some kind of cooking fat; about ½ ounce of macaroni was also issued. For those registered, the communal "victory kitchens" offered a daily meal; typical menus were:

MONDAY: *vegetable soup*
TUESDAY: *dried egg*
WEDNESDAY: *old goat boiled*

On this diet the civilian ration was reduced to 1,200 calories a day, about half the theoretical, minimum subsistence level. On the black market eggs now cost 7s each. Clothes too were a great problem, no cotton could be obtained to mend or patch garments, and many began to suffer from cold. The cumulative effect of this was that large sections of the community were too weak even to go to the shelters during air raids. Tuberculosis also became prevalent. Morale, too, was affected by the ghastly sense of boredom that afflicts all those enduring a long and harsh siege. The *Times of Malta* still did its best to keep up the spirits of the British troops by publishing the English football results regularly on Sundays: its usual size was only four small pages.

After Montgomery's great victory at El Alamein early in November, Rommel's army began its long retreat to Tunisia. Malta was now safe from the enemy. But it was again a race against time, and when 4 merchant ships sailed into Valetta on November 20, the island had only 14 days of food left! After nearly two and a half years of endurance Malta's second great siege was finished. Once again the island had defied a more powerful adversary and had not only survived, but also continued to hit back with great effect for most of the time it was being besieged.

This siege had a magnificent and unexpected sequel. In September 1943, 5 battleships, 8 cruisers, over one dozen destroyers, and many smaller naval vessels streamed into the Grand Harbor and dropped anchor there. This great concourse of warships was the Italian fleet, which, when it surrendered, had been ordered to go to Malta. Malta today flourishes, and most of her scars are gone. But the memory of her Second Great Siege lives on.

Index